801-373-4268   801 319 - 3088
jaynannmpayne@gmail.com
1840 N. 1450 E.
Oak Hills

"WHERE IS OUR HOPE FOR PEACE?"

A RESOURCE FOR FAMILIES COPING WITH SUICIDE

Jaynann M. Payne

By
Jaynann M. Payne
& Dr. Rick H.

Foreword by Richard C. Ferre, M.D.

This publication was made possible by a generous donation from William H. and Patricia Child.

ISBN: 1-57636-129-2
2nd Printing, 2003

Published and Distributed by
Hidden Treasures Foundation,
2550 Washington Blvd. #103,
Ogden UT 84401
M.C. Printing
2227 Larsen Parkway, Provo UT 84606,

Cover painting *"The Light Of The World"* by Gregg Olsen,
Used by permission of Millpond Licensing
310 Center Court, Venice, Florida 34292-3500.

WHERE IS OUR HOPE FOR PEACE?
A RESOURCE FOR FAMILIES COPING
WITH SUICIDE

TABLE OF CONTENTS

FOREWORD BY DR. RICHARD C. FERRE, M.D.   vi-viii

INTRODUCTION: PERSPECTIVE FROM THE PAST
- By Jaynann M. Payne   1

CHAPTER

1.   **THE PROBLEM OF SUICIDE**   5

2.   **WHY SUICIDE?**   7

"One Flame Burning Out . . .and Another One Lit"
–By "Kathy"   10

"Let Go and Let God: One Day At A Time."
–By "Guerry"   15

3.   **HEALING AND HOPE**   23

"Bearing This Special Grief of Suicide"
-- By Father Arnaldo Pangrazzi   23

4.   **THE HEALING PROCESS**
-- By Benjamin E. Payne   29

THE FIVE PHASES OF GRIEF:

5.   **DENIAL AND SHOCK**   31

*"It seems so unreal—suicide happens to other
people, not me!"* --By Jean Hall   31

"I was in shock. I couldn't believe my son was dead."
--By Maxine Zawodniak   36

Understanding the Healing Process: Denial & Shock   42

6.   **ANGER AND BLAME**   45

"Most of all, I felt anger at God." --By Arlene Ball   45

"The Bishop's Son." --By "Thomas"   56

Understanding the Healing Process: Anger   60

7.   **GUILT AND BARGAINING**   65

"I needed to work through my feelings of guilt."
--By Marilyn Harris   65

"I suffer the pains of guilt." --By Laura Toomey   72

Understanding the Healing Process: Guilt and
Bargaining   78

8.   **DEPRESSION AND LONELINESS**   83

"Depression – a cause and an effect of suicide"
--By "Shirley"   83

"What's the point?" Erica --By Bill   92

Understanding the Healing Process: Depression
and Loneliness   96

9.   **ACCEPTANCE AND HOPE IN CHRIST**   101

"What I gained from losing Brian."
--By Margie Holmes   101

"Oh Danny Boy." --By Jane Ann Bradford Olsen   108

Understanding the Healing Process: Acceptance
and Hope in Christ --By Benjamin and Heather Payne   123

10.	THE HEALING POWER OF MUSIC	127
	Creative Uses of Grief	132
11.	"COMFORT YOURSELVES TOGETHER"	135
	It's Okay For A Man To Cry --By Margie Holmes	135
	The Special Needs of Children	140
	Spiritual and Emotional Support Systems – How Relatives and Friends Can Help	145
	"Our prayers were answered by loving friends and family who came and shared our sorrow" --By "Elaine"	147
12.	WHERE IS OUR HOPE FOR PEACE?	155
	Hope	156
	The Atonement – An Eternal Perspective --By Jaynann M. Payne	160
	Our Dependence On Christ, The Prince of Peace	162
13.	SPIRITUAL INSIGHTS GAINED ON THE PATHWAY TO PEACE	165
	How They Survived and Found Peace	165
	Working Their Way Through The Grieving Process Gave The Survivors These Comforting Spiritual Insights	166
	A Solitary Way	180
APPENDIX: HELPS AND RESOURCES		183
	Authors	188
	Index	191

ACKNOWLEDGMENTS

First, I am indebted to my husband, Dean W. Payne, for his encouragement and loyal support. His wise counsel has been most helpful.

We acknowledge the contributions and guidance given by Dr. Rick H. and the Hidden Treasures Foundation. We appreciate their interest and support for the book's publication.

Thank you to Margie Holmes who initially encouraged the manuscript and shared several stories with me. Her editorial assistance and insights were valuable.

We are indebted to two of our children for their contributions: Benjamin E. Payne, a licensed clinical social worker, who, with his wife, Heather, wrote several chapters on the healing process. And to our daughter, Rosalie Payne Lines, a busy mother with six children, who helped edit and clarify our initial document.

Thanks to Sharon Huber for her computer expertise.

Appreciation is expressed to Elder C. Max Caldwell, Dr. Richard G. Ellsworth, Dr. Douglas E. Brinley and Elaine Cannon for reading the manuscript and offering invaluable suggestions.

DEDICATION

To the Survivors of Suicide for their courage and candor in sharing heartfelt experiences and their spiritual journey to peace.

FOREWORD

Suicide is a personal and family tragedy that has devastating consequences. Certainly the loss of the creative talents and the cherished association of a loved one cannot be measured. But for the loved ones left behind, the consequences of suicide may last for years. Suicide presents the survivors with the profound challenge of dealing with innumerable unanswered questions including the reasons for suicide, how the survivors judge themselves in relationship to the suicide victim, and the unanswered questions as to how God will judge those who take their lives. These factors help to place in perspective why this tragedy is so profound.

The following essays that comprise this book are intended to help those struggling with the tragedy surrounding a suicide with comfort and, hopefully, some better understanding through the experiences of others who have faced the same challenge. For twenty-five years, I have been a psychiatrist dealing with the distress of severe emotional and mental illness in the lives of my patients. I have been a part of the devastation that these disorders can have in the lives of people. The human brain is the most complex system in the universe. Surely, there is much of God's love for us in these latter-days as evidenced by the enormous outpouring of knowledge about how the neurochemistry of the brain works. We have learned more in the last thirty years than in the previous 6000 years. Great advances have been made in alleviating the symptoms and dysfunction associated with mental illness through medications and psychosocial interventions. However, in spite of advances, professionals in the mental health field are often helpless in preventing suicide in patients. Despite family and science's best efforts, some of our family and friends continue to take their own lives. The World Health Organization estimates that one million people died from suicide during the year

2000. Youth suicide, the third leading cause of death among teenagers and young adults, accounts for more deaths in the United States than all natural causes combined for youth between the ages of 15 to 24. Suicide risk is also high for older people in the United States who have a higher rate of suicide than any other segment of the population. In 1998 the rate of suicide for white males 85 and older was six times the national age adjusted rate. These are alarming statistics. No segment of the population is immune to this problem and members of the Church of Jesus Christ of Latter-day Saints are no different.

The challenging question as to why these statistics are increasing and why individuals would commit suicide is complex. There exist no easy answers. The majority of scientific research points to the factors of biological illness interacting with psychosocial and environmental stressors in the individuals who eventually take their lives. The presence of mental illness, especially depression and bipolar disorder, are seen in the vast majority of those who become the victims of suicide. These illnesses are not chosen, but are the result of the complex expression of biologic genetic predisposition and environmental stress.

Brain disorders are no respecter of persons. Therefore, although we may not know exactly in any one situation why a particular person took his or her life, we should understand that they were dealing with intense emotional distress, which overcame their ability to cope rationally. This should give us pause to withhold our judgment as to their standing with God, and look to the healing power of the spirit to help us find comfort rather than cause.

What does a Latter-day Saint family do when confronted by the loss of a loved one to suicide? Where does a grieving parent or spouse turn when there is so little to comfort them and so many unanswered questions? This book, *"Where is Our Hope for Peace? A Resource for Families Coping with Suicide,"* is offered as a source of comfort and hope. Personal stories from survivors provide insight for those surviving the tragedy of suicide. Suggestions are made from professional and personal experience to help survivors cope. This book does not pretend to have all the answers or to exhaust the subject, but to begin a dialogue with the reader that may help the person feel less alone in the struggle.

In the Book of Mormon, Nephi struggling with the many unanswered questions in life, responds with this observation: "I know that he loveth His children; nevertheless, I do not know the meaning of all things." (I Nephi 11:17) Certainly, we "do not know the meaning of all things," -- the pain, suffering, the reasons, the outcome for those who commit suicide, but we do know that God loves all his children and that He will do justly and show mercy through His great wisdom and compassion to those that suffer. We likewise can take hope from His great mercy and seek peace in the comfort of His spirit. He loves us, each of us. He loves all His children, including those who end their life by taking it.

Dr. Richard C. Ferre, M.D.
Associate Clinical Professor of Psychiatry
University of Utah, School of Medicine

Introduction

PERSPECTIVE FROM THE PAST

By Jaynann M. Payne

**"There are always two parties to a death;
the person who dies and the survivors who
are bereaved and in the apportionment of
suffering, the survivor takes the brunt."
--Arnold Toynbee**

In 1849, Sarah Evans Jeremy, a Welsh Mormon immigrant traveled to America on the ship Buena Vista with her husband and four children. Their destination was Zion. As they sailed up the Mississippi, cholera broke out. One-third of the 248 Saints became ill and many died. All three of Sarah's little girls died in one night and were buried along the banks of the Mississippi River in a small wooden box. Only Thomas, nine years old, was left. When I read of the trials my ancestors endured, I am deeply touched by their courage and testimonies.

Today we travel through an equally hostile and dangerous environment in the 21st century. We mourn loved ones who were victims of depression, drugs, and suicide, instead of cholera, hunger, and exposure. The suicide of a loved one is possibly the most difficult test for survivors to endure in any time or place. Feelings of failure, unanswered questions, and the terrible stigma are among the experiences survivors typically have. When a loved one commits suicide, those who have invested years of love and caring concern feel abandoned and rejected.

As shocking and heartbreaking as it is to learn of the suicide of someone we know, it is difficult for most of us to understand the emotional and spiritual chaos that is thrust upon the surviving families. Family members and other loved ones are referred to as "survivors" for a reason: They must now survive one of the greatest tragedies life has to offer. Part of that challenge is answering the questions, "Why?" "What do we do now?" and "How can we go on?" In the book, *Where Is Our Hope For Peace? A Resource for Families Coping with Suicide,* we have brought together a variety of stories of those who have confronted suicide. Like the pioneers, they have come to know God in their extremities. Their stories are sacred. They are courageous persons who would like others to understand more about suicide and its effect on families.

The purpose of this book is fourfold. The **first** is to understand "Why suicide?" Two personal stories of members of The Church of Jesus Christ of Latter-day Saints (LDS) who have attempted suicide share insights into their minds and hearts to show how such a tragedy can happen.

Second, the phases of healing typically experienced by survivors of suicide are reviewed. The five phases are:

> Denial and shock
> Anger and blame
> Guilt and bargaining
> Depression and loneliness
> Acceptance and hope in Christ

We also discuss resources of support and comfort to survivors; ideas to help surviving children to heal and suggest some differences between men and women in the grieving and healing process.

The **third** purpose is to share the experiences of some Latter-day Saints who have coped with suicide. Each chapter includes a personal story. The survivors who tell their stories want to give comfort and encouragement to those who suffer from the tragic death of a family member. We admire them for their candor and sincerity in disclosing their innermost thoughts and feelings. They have learned important truths by going through this harrowing experience.

The **fourth** purpose is to emphasize the crucial mission of Christ and His ability to heal and provide comfort. The effects of suicide are devastating, but the survivors who shared their stories learned that the way to wholeness was to place their hands in the hand of the Lord. They trusted Him to pull them through. Their belief in the reality of God's love and Christ's Atonement provided a lifeline on their journey to peace.

No one is immune to this tragedy. Persons of all ages die of suicide; men and women, teenagers, even young children; the rich as well as the poor; active members of the Church and those who are not. Elder M. Russell Ballard, speaking of suicide, recognized that members of the Church struggle with this tragedy and the taking of one's life leaves family members and friends to cope with years of confusion and terrible pain. The survivors struggle with feelings of almost unbearable grief, guilt, anger and rejection. *(The Ensign,* "Suicide: Some things we know, and some we do not," October, 1987; © *2000* by Intellectual Reserve, Inc.*)*

One thing we do know is that the Lord has prepared spiritual aides to support us in our times of trial. In addition to the scriptures, prayer and priesthood blessings, there is the healing power of beautiful music. A favorite LDS hymn, *Where Can I Turn For Peace?* by Emma Lou Thayne and Joleen Meredith, speaks eloquently to those who suffer from the tragedies and contradictions of life. This lovely hymn has brought peace and comfort to some of the survivors of suicide. The hymn, (page 129) reads:

WHERE CAN I TURN FOR PEACE?

Where can I turn for peace?
Where is my solace
When other sources cease to make me whole?
When with a wounded heart, anger, or malice
I draw myself apart, searching my soul?

Where, when my aching grows,
Where, when I languish,
Where, in my need to know, where can I run?

Where is the quiet hand to calm my anguish?
Who, who can understand? He, only One.

He answers privately, reaches my reaching
In my Gethsemane, Savior and Friend.
Gentle the peace he finds for my beseeching.
Constant he is and kind,
Love without end.

(Hymns of The Church of Jesus Christ of Latter-day Saints, p. 129, by Emma Lou Thayne and Joleen Meredith, © 1985 Intellectual Reserve Incorporated, Used by permission)

Where Is Our Hope For Peace? relies heavily on personal stories from Latter-day Saints who have experienced the tragedy of suicide. We have related the stories to Latter-day Saint teachings and doctrines. Nevertheless, individual experiences of Church members do not determine Church policy or doctrine related to suicide. Neither the book nor its authors speak on behalf of The Church of Jesus Christ of Latter-day Saints. We simply share our experiences, thoughts, and feelings as members of the Church who have been united by a common journey to healing and hope. This book is offered as a resource to others who are sorrowing over a suicide so they will know they are not alone in their search for peace.

Chapter 1

THE PROBLEM OF SUICIDE

Art Linkletter, a famous television personality and author, said: "The word *suicide* is without doubt one of the most dreadful expressions in the English language. People wince at the sound of it, and avoid using it to describe the tragic death it implies. Leprosy and cancer are spoken of in the same hushed tones. And yet it must be faced squarely and discussed openly because it has become one of the leading causes of death among both the young and the very old in this country. My own personal experience with it is still a nightmare. The death of my nineteen-year-old daughter, Diane, after experimenting with LSD changed my life and the lives of everyone in my family... Since then I have counseled with many grieving parents who have sought me out because they know that only those who have experienced this loss can understand its depth and its consequences in a family. We need to know more about the complexity of the decision to take one's own life."

THE STIGMA OF SUICIDE

Suicide is a historical fact. The stigma attached to suicide has a history arising in the Bible. In the early Christian era there was an epidemic of suicides. Life was difficult and many believers were eager to enter heaven. The church wanted to stop it. Saint Augustine proclaimed suicide a sin, the sin of self-murder, and Thomas Aquinas convinced the church to declare suicide a mortal sin with eternal damnation as the punishment. Laws were put into effect inflicting harsh punishments to anyone attempting suicide and the government took all property belonging to the victim. The body was not allowed a proper Christian burial and the surviving families were ridiculed with contempt, disgust and scorn. Often they had to move away from their home. The stigma of suicide was disgrace, dishonor, humiliation and shame. Even talking about suicide became forbidden.

Laws have slowly changed and although there aren't any legal consequences in our country today, the stigma and shame are slow to be erased. People have no idea how much pain they can inflict with insensitive remarks. Many churches and synagogues are working to change these attitudes but even most professionals such as religious leaders, teachers, nurses, doctors, and counselors, have not received sufficient education about suicide or the grieving process of the survivors.

For members of The Church of Jesus Christ of Latter-day Saints, the *Encyclopedia of Mormonism* gives this comfort and guidance to survivors:

> Suicide and attempted suicide are painful and dramatic aspects of human behavior, but it does not mean that they should not be dealt with in terms of the same basic principles as those applicable in understanding and managing any other aspect of human behavior. Thus, principles associated with concepts of agency, accountability, atonement, eternal life, immortality, resurrection, and family establish the frame of reference Latter-day Saints use to guide their responses to such behaviors as they occur.

> The body of a person who has committed suicide is not dishonored. If the person has been endowed (in the temple) and otherwise is in good standing with the Church, the body may be buried in temple clothes. Normal funeral procedures are followed. *(Encyclopedia of Mormonism, Suicide, p.* 1422 ©1992 by Macmillan Publishers Inc.)

Chapter 2

WHY SUICIDE?

Why would anyone willingly hasten or cause his or her own death? Perhaps the worst torture for a survivor is thinking, "Why did he do it? What was she feeling? What could he have been thinking? What could we have done to prevent it?" These questions reflect a desire to understand the feelings and motivations of the person who has died, a sometimes desperate, but normal need to make sense of a senseless act. It is normal to struggle with trying to understand until you no longer need to know why or until you are satisfied with partial answers.

Suicide does not happen because of a single event or series of events--not rage at a parent, not a divorce, not any single event. Many persons have had tragic and challenging experiences and they have not taken their own lives. Suicides typically have multiple causes. Other forces drive those who commit suicide after a particular event. In the end, it is something internal that causes the suicide, and not something done by the survivors. The suicide victim may say some harsh things prior to death or blame others in a suicide note. Survivors, no doubt, have done or said things that they regret. That happens in all relationships. But our words and acts do not make a suicide victim. We cannot "make" another person commit suicide. For us, there is a solution we can live with to every problem if we try hard enough, but to one who commits suicide, the only solution seems to be death.

Most suicide attempts are reactions to intense feelings of loneliness, worthlessness, helplessness, and depression. Mental health professionals generally agree that people who took their own lives felt trapped by what they felt was a hopeless situation. They felt isolated and cut off from life and friendships. Even if no physical illness was present, suicide victims felt intense pain, anguish, and hopelessness. They probably weren't choosing death as much as choosing to end their unbearable pain.

WARNING SIGNS

How can you tell if someone is thinking about committing suicide? Three-quarters of all suicides gave some warning of their intentions to a family member or friend. Be concerned if your loved one:

- Talks about life as "hopeless" or complains of feeling "helpless"
- Withdraws from friends, family, and regular activities
- Takes unnecessary risks
- Sleeping habits change – sleeping a lot or not sleeping well
- Talks about death or complains that "life is not worth living"
- Is suddenly more rebellious, angry, violent, or moody.
- Neglects his or her personal appearance
- Uses drugs or alcohol
- Noticeable weight loss or weight gain
- Complains of feeling "rotten inside"
- Becomes suddenly cheerful after a bout of depression
- Gives away prized possessions
- Threatens suicide

No one completely understands the complex puzzle of suicide. There are many factors that can lead to the fatal act. The two personal accounts that follow illustrate some of the major factors accompanying suicide, particularly depression and substance abuse, elements common even to Latter-day Saints who die of suicide.

Depression is the most pervasive contributing factor to a person taking his or her own life. Deep depression entails a sense of engulfing despair, including the belief that no one could ever understand the suicidal person's suffering. This belief leads to isolation, hopelessness, and a sense of futility about communicating with anyone. Those who commit suicide are desperately unhappy. They may not reveal the problems about which they feel so unhappy--alcoholism, rejection in an important relationship, a business failure, or a spiritual conflict. They may have a mental or physical disorder. They feel incapable of connecting to anyone and they have no hope for the future. The black cloud of depression distorts the rational mind so that only the painful present seems real and death seems to them to be the only escape. To those who love the victim, death is a permanent solution to what should be a temporary problem, but to the suicidal person, it seems to be the only solution. Kathy's story illustrates the overwhelming feelings that can occur because of depression.

Some suicidal persons hope someone will stop them and will give clear messages of their intent. Others hope to be saved and helped, but do not know how to ask in a way that will be heard, understood and acted upon. Still others are complete in their resolve and will fool everyone. Guerry, whose story follows that of Kathy, is an example of someone who successfully hid his intent. His story also illustrates the role that drugs and alcohol can play.

One Flame Burning Out...And Another One Lit

By Kathy

When I was asked to write this story, I found myself procrastinating for a long time. It was painful. Even years later it was hard for me to accept and understand that part of my life. Eventually, I felt the need to finish my story in the hope that I could help others understand, in a small way, what it is like to be willing to take one's own life.

I came from an abusive background. I remember little but fear and trying to stay safe, both physically and emotionally. My grandmother was my only source of security. She had unconditional love for me and was the only spiritual person I knew, but I was only allowed to have her for a short time. My father would not allow anything positive in my life. He cut off our relationship. My grandmother was very well read in the scriptures, a member of Utah Daughters of the Pioneers, a teacher and an actress in many Church plays. She gave me the only foundation in my faith that I had.

My parents expected me to go to church, but they never considered going with me. I hardly ever missed church because it was a refuge. I always thought how nice it would be if I were part of a family that went to church - like the others in my ward. As it was, I strove to do what was right because I didn't want to disappoint my grandmother. If I needed to give a talk she would help me by mail. She would send me letters and Church magazines, but I didn't always get them. Those early years of my life were frightening. I was painfully shy. I knew that when I was 18 years old I could see my grandmother when I wanted to, but I guess the Lord had other plans. In my junior year, my grandmother was hit by a car and killed. The only person I knew who wanted the best for me was gone and a part of me died with her.

I got married and within a year and a half I had my first child. I tried to stay close to the Church and finally talked my husband into going to the temple. I thought I would be more accepted by his family and others if we went to the temple. I didn't understand then the right reason to do those things.

My husband and I lived in the same ward I was in while growing up. It seemed difficult for other ward members to accept me as an adult. I felt anger, depression, hurt, and rebellion. I was just trying to fit in. My husband wasn't much support for me. All he cared about was getting more of the pills that took the pain away for him. He continued to smoke but hid it from the ward. Later I learned that he had tried to "hit on" my best friend.

My parents interfered with my life and my marriage, but because of the abuse I experienced as a child, I played the victim role with my parents even as an adult. Then one day I decided I had had enough. The marriage had been nothing but chaos. I was being supported financially more by my parents than my husband. I felt abandoned by the ward members. In fact, I believed my husband received more support than I did at the time. I divorced my husband. I didn't know what I was going to do, but I felt at the time that anything was better than what I had. By this time, I was so angry and confused about everything that I stopped attending church.

Soon I met my second husband. He wasn't active at first, but he was a good man. He told me once, he thought God had arranged for us to meet. We were married for quite some time before we moved to Utah County and I started to go back to Church. I continued to feel a spiritual void. I didn't believe God loved me. I was afraid and I felt so awkward because I had never learned to trust, but I wanted desperately to be a good example to my children.

During this time, I was teaching Church classes and serving in presidencies. I'm sure I looked very good on the outside, but it didn't last. We moved and my husband and I became inactive in the church again. At one point, we had to live with my husband's family. They treated us badly and the children were very unhappy.

It was there that my life started to break down around me. I felt like I had lost control. One of my children was caught shoplifting. My husband and I fought all the time. As the days turned into months I could tell I was dropping into a deep depression, a black, black hole. This darkness is so hard to describe. My thoughts went something like this, "Who wants me? No one. Not my children. Not even my Father in Heaven." I believed my children would be better without me because I couldn't "fix anything." I was convinced I was no good to anyone, least of all myself. I felt that there was no one who would understand what I was "screaming" about inside.

As I look back on those dark days, they are as clear to me as if they were yesterday. One particular day stands out in my memories. I can still see the cold unhappy room. It had drab furnishings and one large window. The walls were painted light brown. I was upstairs sitting on the edge of the bed with a gun in my hands. I believed that dying was the only way I could solve my problems. I had the distinct feeling of separating from my body like there were two people. One person was holding the gun, the other person was sitting beside me. I felt black depression. The pain was so strong. The emptiness, the aching, the numb feelings were so powerful that I wanted to die. Remembering how much pain I had then, hurts terribly.

I know that people want to say things to those who are considering suicide like, "Get over it", "Nothing can be that bad", "Just tell yourself something positive", "Pray and go to church", or "Don't be stupid." I'm a licensed counselor now and if I'm not careful, I begin to think it is that easy and say some of the same things. But for me at that time, the idea of wanting to escape and kill myself seemed far more powerful than anything anyone could say. Suicide seemed like the solution, not the problem. I don't know how long I sat there on the bed. At one point the gun was loaded and I had it pointed at my head. All I had to do was move one finger and it would have been over. I don't know how much time passed, but I put the gun back in the drawer. Then I called my doctor and tried to explain what had taken place. Within the hour, the doctor had a social work therapist call me and I started the healing process.

Professional counseling, medication, and learning of God's love for me helped me begin to come out of the black hole. About one year later my husband became very ill and died. The children missed him very much. I went to a community college and eventually completed my bachelor's and master's degrees. I still had a spiritual void. I didn't feel like killing myself anymore, but something was still missing. I decided to go back to Church for myself this time. The flame was rekindled as I began to realize more and more that God did have a plan for me and that He did love me. Romans 8: 35, 38-39 says:

> "Who shall separate us from the love of Christ? Shall tribulation, or distress, or persecution, or famine, or nakedness, or peril, or sword? . . . For I am persuaded, that neither death, nor life, not angels, nor principalities, nor powers, nor things present nor things to come, nor height, nor depth, nor any other creature, shall be able to separate us from the love of God."

Now I know regardless of where I am or the condition I'm in, God loves me. I thank my Heavenly Father that my life has never been as devastating as it was that day sitting on the bed with a gun. I continue to work on my personal issues. I gain strength from going to the temple and my testimony has grown so much. I bear my testimony that if we continue to keep an open mind, keep communication open with our Heavenly Father, He will be willing to guide us to the right answers. If we listen. If we knock. Doctrine and Covenants 66:9 says: "Be patient in affliction. Ask, and you shall receive; knock, and it shall be opened unto you."

Today I am a therapist. I love my job. There are so many times I ask my Heavenly Father for guidance in my job because I know the people I work with daily are His children. Many times the spirit has guided my thoughts or my words. Periodically, I see someone like I used to be, depressed, in darkness and wanting to die. I understand. I've often wondered why others pull the trigger and I didn't. I don't know. I know God loves me. My life is precious. In the next life, perhaps I can understand all of the "whys and the hows" of what happened to me that horrible time. For now, I live my life so that I will be prepared for death when it comes on life's terms - and not mine.

POEM

Who never mourned hath never known
What treasures grief reveals,
The sympathies that humanize,
The tenderness that heals.
The power to look beyond the veil,
And learn the heavenly lore,
Will teach the key to life's mysteries,
So dark to us before.

-Author Unknown

Let Go And Let God: One Day At A Time

By Guerry

The story of my nearly successful suicide in October 1992 is hard to relate, but if it can help others understand this insane behavior, it's worth the effort. Some folks, when they hear my life story, might think I've had a difficult life. Maybe I have, I've learned a lot about God, living, and myself, from my challenges. It's taken me quite a few years to learn how to want to live. Let me begin my story by sharing a thought from Elder Richard G. Scott, who said, "Although the Lord is able to cure illnesses or disabilities or even raise the dead, He generally allows us to experience adversity that we may grow and improve our character. We should ask ourselves questions such as: What does the Lord want me to learn from this hard and painful experience? Is there something I need to do or change? Is there someone I need to serve? Through earnest prayer and pondering, we may come to understand more about the Lord's timetable and His purposes for our lives." (The *Ensign,* "Obtaining Help From the Lord." November 1991, p. 84-85 © 1991 by Intellectual Reserve Inc.)

Let me tell you about the challenges I have been asked to overcome. I was born and raised in what I thought was a good Christian home. However, my mother and father both used alcohol pretty heavily. I was taught quite clearly the sanctity of life. My Father was a veteran of both World Wars, and had to take the lives of enemy soldiers. When he spoke of this he taught me the seriousness of taking a life. The pain and soberness in his eyes made a lasting impression. As a young man, the thought of taking the life of another, much less my own life, was not even a consideration.

As a Latter-day Saint, I promised God not to partake of alcohol and drugs and I had also promised my father not to do so. My father unexpectedly passed away when I was young. Less than six months after he died, I was drinking along with my friends. It was a very significant failure in my life. I knew better.

Nevertheless, at the time I thought it was a traditional right of passage toward real manhood to drink and party. Growing up in an alcoholic home and having many heavy drinkers for progenitors, I believe I was predisposed genetically to addiction. I adopted the thinking and behavior that children of alcoholics typically come away with - people-pleasing, perfectionism, black and white thinking, and over-achieving. Consequently, I drank and used drugs heavily between the ages of 14 and about 19. I never knew what it was like to do things in moderation. If one was good, then three or four was even better.

I was about 18 when I was converted to The Church of Jesus Christ of Latter Day Saints. The missionaries brought a message of hope that rang true. Nevertheless, it took me several months after my baptism to quit alcohol and drug use. I subsequently fought in the Vietnam War in the Marine Corps, but I never drank or used drugs despite encouragement and many opportunities to do so.

After my discharge, I went to BYU, married my wife, got my bachelor's degree in Social Work, and then worked as a pharmaceutical sales representative. My wife and I were active Church members, sincerely trying our best to do what was right and to build the Kingdom. As a 29-year-old bishop, I worked with people in my ward who had serious problems. I tried to help them overcome their problems by relying on the Savior and feeling good about themselves. Their self-esteem seemed to improve and they could feel God's love. But I learned later in my life that I couldn't help myself in the same way.

I had five children under age six by the time I was released as bishop. My expectations for my family and myself were idealistic and rigid. As pressures and expectations increased, so did my tension and anxiety. Migraines became a problem and I worried excessively about my problems and the future. I eventually noticed the headache medication helped me with the emotional pain as well as the physical pain. By the time I was in my late 30's I began to have thoughts of taking my own life. I was experiencing a great deal of shame and emotional pain, much of which resulted from substance abuse and the behaviors arising out of it.

This continued to escalate over the next ten years until I began drinking again. I became a full-blown addict/alcoholic, completely out of control. Finances, job, relationships, and spirituality suffered as a result. In my mind I was a worthless and despicable person, bringing more and more misery to my loved ones. The people that I claimed to care about were suffering because of my addiction.

By age thirty-nine or forty, I began thinking of specific ways to take my life. Initially, these were just passing thoughts, but as time went on those thoughts began to linger and to be worked out in some detail. I viewed my dying to be a good thing for my family almost from the beginning, because I saw myself as so defective. In my depressed and confused state of mind I felt that a large life insurance benefit would more than offset my loss. It would be like a sacrifice, so my family could live better financially. Rarely did I consider what the widow and the fatherless would go through, even though I had been fatherless in my youth. I think I was just past feeling. Alcohol and pills became less and less effective in taking away my pain. The depression was so bad that I became more and more dysfunctional. Every aspect of my life was going down the tubes. I became so completely absorbed in my physical and emotional pain, my only thoughts were of escaping and finding relief.

Finally, a series of events--more failures and disappointments--drove me to the edge. I set up an accident scene and rehearsed what I would do--accidental death benefits are double that of natural death. The week before I was to follow through with the plan, my son was getting an award at church. For the first and only time I can recall, I considered the effect my death would have on my family. I knew I needed to be there at church when my son received his award so I temporarily postponed taking my life.

Around this time, others seemed to sense my despair. My physician who had been treating me for depression became concerned enough to talk to me specifically about suicide. He had his nurse (whose father had committed suicide) talk to me. He tried with medication, kind words and counsel to make sure I wouldn't go that route. My physician went to great lengths to help me. He tried an intervention along with another physician-friend, my general surgeon who had recently removed part of my stomach due to ulcers. These loving approaches (both subtle and straightforward) that might otherwise have been very effective were too late. I was far more despondent than anyone knew. It seemed to be almost a peaceful feeling to know my life would soon be over. As a skilled manipulator, I smiled and put on a facade that would have convinced anyone that I was OK and would never do such a thing as suicide. Those few who were suspecting I was headed that direction were appeased by my denials.

Problems at home worsened. Finally, my wife became so miserable she asked me to move out for a temporary separation. This was the final straw, the ultimate failure that brought my plans to fruition. There was no doubt in my mind what I was going to do. I don't believe anyone on earth could have stopped me. I'd failed everyone important to me-my family, my friends, my God. All I knew about the gospel, the plan of salvation, all the counsel I gave my ward members and even my own family was of no assistance to me. I went out of town on a business trip, loaded up on pills, and "accidentally" drove off a thousand-foot overlook in Logan Canyon on the late afternoon of October 16, 1992.

I should have died immediately. I was thrown from the car as it tumbled down the mountain. But, it was deer season, and a hunter found my battered body on the side of the mountain only hours after the accident. I was flown to LDS Hospital where I remained in a coma for a few days. While in a coma the miracle continued. I came to know that God loved me. For some reason, I never knew it before, but I knew it now. I was of value to Him and sensed that I had far greater worth than my mortal mind could have ever conceived. I learned that my worth was irrespective of any mortal errors I was or could have been guilty of- much less the relatively minor errors I had so magnified in my own mind. Gradually I came out of the coma and went through head injury rehabilitation therapy. I began a substance abuse treatment program. In treatment, I learned more about my Father in Heaven and the love He has for me. As I sat in that drug rehab center, I realized there was no hope for me if I didn't let God into my life. I learned how to let go and let God and to live one day at a time.

My spiritual rebirth continued when I began to incorporate these truths into my life. There was no way I could face all the problems that were now before me. I knew I would end up trying to kill myself again. And if there was a next time, I knew I wouldn't fail. But, I thought there was hope if I could just let go and let God and live one day at a time.

It has been almost ten years now. I continue to allow God's and others' love into my life. There are still difficult days and I must take antidepressant medications. When people ask me what I learned by driving off that cliff, I personalize the scripture found in the Matthew 6:25-34 to read like this:

Therefore I say unto you Guerry, take no thought for your life, what ye shall eat, or what ye shall drink, nor yet for your body, what ye shall put on. Is not your life more than meat and the body than raiment? Behold the fowls of the air; for they sow not, neither do they reap nor gather into barns; yet, your heavenly Father feedeth them. You, Guerry, are much better than they! Which of you by taking thought can add a cubit unto his stature? And, why take ye thought for raiment? Consider the lilies of the field how they grow; they toil not neither do they spin: And yet I say unto you Guerry, that even Solomon in all his glory was not arrayed like one of these. Wherefore, if God so clothe the grass of the field, which today is and tomorrow is cast into the oven, shall he not much more clothe you, 0 ye of little faith? Therefore, Guerry take no thought saying, what shall you eat? Or what shall you drink? Or, Wherewith all shall ye be clothed. For your heavenly Father knoweth that ye have need of all these things. But seek ye first the Kingdom of God and his righteousness and all these things shall be added unto you. Take therefore no thought for the morrow Guerry, for the morrow shall take thought for the things of itself. Sufficient unto the day is the evil thereof.

I know now that my suicide attempt was a plea for help. I was not only suffering from depression but had an enormous amount of life stress. I couldn't go on any further. As a drug-free recovering addict, I am no longer in danger of harming myself and I enjoy life. Because of the head injury from driving off the cliff, I periodically have problems with memory and concentration, especially when I'm under stress. After all these years because of where I've been, I know more about serenity and "*. . . the peace of God which passeth all understanding.*" (Philippians 4:7) I can give my yoke to Him and if I work my program, my burdens are light. But I have to work at it every day. I can't be casual about my scripture reading, going to the temple, attending support group meetings, or saying my prayers. If I do, and I get discouraged, the thoughts of killing myself come back. It only lasts for a moment, but having been where I've been, it seems that it is always an option, an option I choose not to use.

My message to survivors

If I were to speak to survivors of suicide, I would like you to understand when we attempt suicide we are in an enormous amount of pain and anguish. Many of us are suffering from serious emotional and substance abuse problems at the time. Please, don't be angry with us. Although it ended the way it did, we tried our best. Though we may have failed in your eyes, we really did try to make it work. Because of the depths of despair we were in, we were not thinking of how bad it would hurt you to have us gone. I honestly thought that it would be better for my loved ones without me. That is why I did it! Even if we said it was your fault, it really wasn't. When we say things like that it is just part of our sick thinking. Your loved one who died of suicide would like to tell you something like this:

"Please don't be eaten up with emotional pain worrying about what you might have done to save my life or what you might have done that caused me to take my life. Go on. Let go of me. Let God take care of me. There is one righteous judge who will know my heart and my mind. He loves me. He'll make all the decisions about my accountability, not you or the neighbors or ward members. *Let go and let God.* Think of the reunion that will surely come because of the gospel plan. I'll be there waiting for you. Don't focus on the last few minutes of my death. Remember me for the years we had together: my smiles, my favorite food, my favorite hobby, and all the fun times we had. Things will work out. I'll be okay. You can make it. Just try. *One day at a time.* And if that is too hard try one hour at a time."

Chapter 3

HEALING AND HOPE

"Bearing the Special Grief of Suicide"
By Father Arnaldo Pangrazzi

The suicide of someone you care about is a devastating tragedy. It happens in the best of families and to the best of people, shattering the lives of the shocked survivors. Because you are bewildered by what has happened, you search for whys. A message left may help interpret what went on in the person's mind before the suicide. Yet the painful questions remain: "Why did he do it?" "Was she angry at me?"

You may also be filled with guilt, for suicide seems like not just a loss but also an accusation. You may feel that somehow you did not love enough, or that your relationship was not good enough. You keep rehearsing all the "if onlys": "Why didn't I realize how sick he was?" "If only I had been home on time."

WORKING YOUR WAY THROUGH

Recovery from the suicide of someone close is a monumental task, for the process of mending a broken heart is painful and slow. The road to recovery requires you to accept your feelings, to draw from your inner resources, and to develop positive attitudes toward the past, present, and future. The journey of healing starts with small steps leading from darkness to hope, from death to a renewed commitment to life.

Learn to live with unanswered questions

We do have some clues about why people choose suicide. We know that suicide is often the response to some kind of loss; to real or perceived failure; to physical, psychological, or spiritual pain. The person's problem becomes the only thing that exists, and he or she cannot conceive that life will ever become any better.

But even knowing all this intellectually, you can still feel very confused emotionally. Behind your questions is a broken heart that can't be healed with simple answers. Struggling through the not knowing is extremely difficult. Your whys may never be answered, the puzzle never resolved. People who complete suicide often take with them the mystery of their life and death. You must gradually let go of the whys, accept what has happened, and go on living.

Allow time for bad memories

In the early stages of grief, survivors often experience playback of the suicide scene in their thoughts or in nightmares. You may feel robbed of pleasant memories and oppressed by this replay of the details surrounding the final event. You need to own and deal with these negative images before you can get in touch with your good memories. As the hurt gradually becomes less intense, positive feelings will surface and become more frequent and longer lasting.

Acknowledge your feelings of anger

Instinctively, survivors tend to reject the way their loved one chose to end his or her life. They may resent the deceased for checking out of the relationship on his or her own terms. They may also resent God for having allowed this to happen, or others for not preventing it. Anger is an investment. We never get angry at someone we do not care about. Anger, therefore, is not the opposite of love but a dimension of it-a sign of a love deeply wounded.

"Give sorrow words .... the grief that does not speak whispers the o'er-fraught heart, and bids it break."
--William Shakespeare

Your anger can help you survive and reenter life or it can become destructive; it depends on how you channel it. You might try discussing your anger with an understanding friend, or talking about it with God, or writing a letter expressing it to the deceased. Ultimately, anger needs to be healed through a willingness to forgive.

Turn guilt into forgiveness

Most survivors blame themselves for what they did or did not do. They have the sense of something left unfinished, something suddenly interrupted. They find it hard to let go of their rescue fantasies. Guilt accompanies many of our experiences of powerlessness and imperfection. It can paralyze and demoralize us, or we can transform it into self-forgiveness and a greater capacity for loving those that are still around us.

Healing takes place when you realize that you cannot judge your yesterday with the knowledge of today, that love alone may not be enough to save another's life, that there are limits to your power and responsibility, that you were not the only influence in the life of the deceased.

Accept the loneliness

Loneliness is the price we pay for loving. When a loved person dies, a part of us dies too. To some degree, the loneliness may last a lifetime, because no one can ever replace that person. We feel the keen disappointment of not having that special person there to share in the family's changes, surprises, sorrows. Loneliness can help you realize the depths of your love. From it, you can learn to become more sensitive to other's losses and to turn to God, who is always there.

Draw from your own spiritual resources

You may be struggling with questions like "Will God forgive her, or has he condemned her to hell?" While the act of suicide continues to be objectively wrong, contemporary theologians emphasize that individual circumstances may make it subjectively guiltless. Those who take their life may be so disturbed that they act compulsively; their perception of reality may be so distorted that their responsibility is greatly reduced. Only God knows what is in the heart of each person.

Obviously, it does not take your grief away simply believing that God will view your loved one's action compassionately. But faith will help you live with your loss and grieve it well. And it will help you discover redeeming values in the midst of your suffering. Trust that God will sustain you through the stages of your bereavement.

Rebuild your self-esteem

The suicide of a friend or loved one is a terrible blow to one's self-image. Rationally or irrationally, the survivors may feel judged by the community for having failed. They may feel that the suicide is a disgrace to the family or the school or even the community. Some have a strong urge to escape to a place where they are not known. And, unfortunately, the shame many survivors feel keeps them from acknowledging the suicide and talking about it-an important part of the recovery process. After the shattering experience of a suicide, you need to pick up the pieces, reaffirm your commitment to life, and rebuild confidence in yourself.

Be patient with yourself

Remember that time, by itself, does not heal. It is how you use the time that's important. When you can stare less frequently at the past and can recognize the value of small steps, you develop a framework within which the passage of time makes the loss not easier, but at least less hard.

Reach out to others

You can choose to let your brokenness defeat you, or you can decide to get up and get going. Once you have the courage to place your hurt, your sensitivity, and your compassion at the service of others, you have discovered the key to help yourself. For when pain is used to reach out to others, it becomes creative and transforming love.

TAKE HEART

Suicide leaves deep scars on the survivors. But there is no turning back: You cannot change what has happened. You can, however, change your outlook from backward to forward, from death to life. Those who have experienced the suicide of a loved one can learn to let go of blaming themselves or the deceased for their unhappiness. They can learn to live for themselves, and to take responsibility for their own future. They can emerge from their sorrow with a profound appreciation for the solidarity they have experienced with others, and with a deep awareness of the beauty and fragility of life. And they can begin to see life not so much as a problem to be solved, but as a mystery to be discovered each day.

Father Arnaldo Pangrazzi resides in Rome as the international coordinator for ministry for the Order of St. Camillus. He has conducted seminars and founded support groups for the bereaved, cancer patients, and suicide survivors. Reprinted with permission by One Caring Place, Abbey Press, © 1988, St. Meinrad Archabbey, IN 47577. (*SOS -Survivors of Suicide Newsletter*, Jan-Feb 1997 - Idaho Falls, ID)

Chapter 4

THE HEALING PROCESS

By Benjamin E. Payne

Suicide is a traumatic loss -- sudden, unexpected, and often violent. The grief it causes is intense and prolonged. Survivors of suicide are left a painful legacy, not one they chose, but one that was forced upon them by their loved one. In many ways, suicide is one of the most difficult deaths to mourn. As you mourn the death of your friend or loved one, you probably feel a sense of betrayal. You have invested years of caring, love and patience with the deceased. Suddenly you are abandoned and rejected. You may think, "How could she do this to me?" "Couldn't he think about the children? Weren't we enough for him?" Ironically, the survivors experience many of the same feelings their loved ones experienced *before* taking their lives. This part of the book is about those feelings survivors often encounter.

None of us can escape the problems and strife of mortality. The very word mortality reminds us that this life is temporary and that there is an eternal perspective that we do not yet understand. Nevertheless, we do understand those feelings survivors typically have when a loved one dies. Dr. Elisabeth Kubler-Ross is known for her research and strategies of care for the dying. In her book *On Death and Dying* (Collier Books, 1997) she determined that family members, who have lost a loved one, go through several stages of grief. This grieving process is particularly noticeable for those dealing with the suicide of a loved one. We have adapted Dr. Kubler-Ross' stages of grief here discussing them as the "phases of healing." The emotions and behavior expected of someone healing from the suicide of a loved one are:

♦ *Denial and shock*
♦ *Anger and blame*
♦ *Guilt and bargaining*
♦ *Depression and loneliness*
♦ *Acceptance and hope in Christ*

These five phases are important to emotional, mental, and spiritual recovery of the survivors. Each person's grief is individual and therefore the process may differ in sequence and duration, but all will experience these phases. The grieving and healing process can last months or years. Children who experience the loss of someone they love will also go through a healing cycle similar to adults. The grieving process is a normal and natural process of dealing with the death of a loved one, but it is still very painful.

The phases of healing may overlap or proceed in a jagged pattern of forward progress, then retreat to an earlier phase, then forward again. No two people will react alike, and the same person will not react in the same way to every loss. However, each phase is typically experienced to a peak of intensity before it can be resolved.

Normal grief is healthy and under favorable environmental conditions, will lead not only to recovery, but also to growth and positive change. As a survivor, your wounds can heal. You can recover, but not through the passage of time alone. The old adage "Time heals all" is not true for all suicide survivors. Some survivors refuse to work through the healing process for many years, but the pain must be faced for healing to occur. In some cases, the additional support of professional counseling and medication will help survivors to find joy in life again.

Chapter 5

DENIAL AND SHOCK

"It seems so unreal-Suicide happens to other people, not me!"

MATT'S STORY

By Jean Hall

It was May 17, 1992. We went to church that Sunday afternoon. We've always attended church together. We were very active in the LDS Church. My husband Bill, and our sons Jim, Mike, Jason, and Matthew went out after church, returning home later that evening. Matt was the youngest son. It was school the next day so I went to bed with everyone else. I was very tired so they all came into my room for goodnight hugs and kisses. When I realized that Matt had not come in I hollered to him "Matt, I love you, Good night." I don't know if he heard me. Later that night I heard a noise, and went outside to investigate. I noticed that Mike's truck was gone. I went in the house to see if he had gone out but Mike was there. He got up and we drove around to see if we could find his truck. As we were driving home, we spotted the truck parked in a vacant lot across the street from Matt's best friend's house next to some construction equipment. There was a 22 rifle in it, a spotlight, and some bullets on the seat, but we didn't see anyone around. There were no keys in the truck, so we drove home to get a set. We learned later that Matt and Nathaniel were hiding behind the equipment.

When we got home I went to Matt's room. The light was on and he was gone. I was amazed. I just couldn't believe that he would or could take the truck. I didn't think he could drive it. He was very small for his age. We decided he was probably with his friend Nathaniel, who is a lot taller than Matt and could drive the truck. My husband and I went back to the vacant lot. The truck was gone. We drove around town in the fields searching. Bill and

I went in one car, Mike and Jim went in another. Jason stayed home with our daughter, 11 year old Colleen. We searched for hours. As the night wore on, I became very frightened. At 4:00 a.m., I took Bill home so that he could get some sleep before work. The rest of us kept going over and over every street in town and then the fields.

I was frantic. I had a very bad feeling about Matt. This was so unlike him and I just could not understand what was wrong. We continued searching until 7:00 a.m. By this time I was pretty sure that something terrible had happened. We started calling Matt's friends to see if he was with any of them. The whole situation was just unreal. I was beginning to fall apart. Even now, writing this brings back the extreme fear I felt that night.

We were still searching when Jim found us and told us Matt had shown up at home. We went straight home. As I got out of the car, I had a sick feeling come over me. Jim said that he had yelled at Matt and sent him to his room. When I went into his room, the window was open and the screen was pushed out. Matt was gone. We assumed that he was upset and was afraid of getting in trouble, so he had taken off on foot. We searched again for Matt.   We decided to come home, thinking that he would eventually return. We felt like the crisis was over as far as his safety was concerned.

Jim went to work and Mike and Jason went downstairs to sleep. Bill was getting ready for work. Mike came upstairs to say he had heard a noise in the closet under the stairs. It was where the guns were stored. Mike stayed upstairs with me and Bill went to check. Something told me not to go with him. The next thing I remember is Bill running up the stairs screaming, "Call 911! Matt has been shot!" I don't remember much other than falling to the floor. I was in shock. I couldn't believe it. The house seemed to come alive with people everywhere. I wanted to be with Matt, but I couldn't make myself go downstairs. I remember a police officer telling me that Matt was still alive and the ambulance was taking him.

Matt died on the way to the hospital. He had been shot in his forehead on the right side. Even as I write this, it seems so unreal to me. This happens to other people, not me. I sincerely thought the Lord would never let me lose a child, especially to suicide. I had many trials as a child and young woman, and I honestly believed that losing a child was something the Lord would not make me endure. I was wrong.

The next few days were so hectic. The house was filled with people. I can't really remember too much. I just remember the pain, a pain so intense that I have not yet found a way to deal with it when it comes back. I still couldn't believe Matt was dead.

Matthew died May 18, 1992, a Monday morning. I didn't see him until Wednesday afternoon. When I saw him at the mortuary he looked like he was sleeping. The bullet hole was so small that Bill had to show me where it was. He was a beautiful child with blond hair. For some reason, I felt much better after I saw and touched him. I spent a lot of time with Matt over the next day and a half but I still had difficulty accepting that it was my son in the casket. As I looked at Matt, I thought about my own death. I wanted to be with him more than anything, but I felt guilty about that because I love my husband and other children too. I felt torn between Matt in the spirit world and my family here on earth.

The funeral was beautiful. The speakers and the music gave us great peace and I felt Matt's spirit there. School was let out for the funeral. Matt was dressed in his black dress pants and his favorite green turtleneck and sweater. You rarely saw Matt without his hat. He had it on when he shot himself. It had a few blood spots on it so I washed it and put it on him. I also put his pocketknife in his pocket. Now when I think of Matt in his casket, I feel that he is warm and comfortable and safe. I get comfort even now from knowing I took care of him like he would have wanted.

To lose a child is the worst thing that can happen to a mother, but to lose a child to suicide is even more difficult. There are so many questions. I don't know if Matt killed himself or if it was an accident. Only God really knows. There was no note. Matt seemed to me to have been a happy, loved, and well-adjusted

14-year-old. But of course, I'm his mother. The events of the night before Matt's death make his death look like suicide, but I just don't know. Even though it has been several years since his death, I still don't want to believe that he shot himself. I want very much to believe that it was an accident. I've finally concluded that it wouldn't ease the pain if I did know. Matthew would still be dead and we would still have this gaping hole in our family.

After the funeral, I felt a need to touch him, to smell him, and to see him walking up the road from school. I thought often to myself, "If I could have just one more touch." The first few months after his death I cried constantly. I was totally useless as a wife or mother. The most difficult thing for me to deal with was not having Matthew home with us. I missed his awful looking bathrobe and the Legos spread over the floor. I couldn't yell at him to turn his radio off at night. Sometimes I even thought I saw him. But then reality would return and drown me in pain. At the time I thought this empty place could never be filled.

I visited Matt's grave every day. I knew in my heart, that it was just his body in the casket and he was in the spirit world. My beliefs in the spirit world and the resurrection gave me some peace. Yet, I wondered why I felt such a strong need to seek Matt in the cemetery if he really wasn't there. Nonetheless, I found peace there. It just seemed to be the only physical part of him that I had left.

I still visit his grave. It's there that I can touch the ground under which he lies. I can touch his name on the granite headstone. I get a great deal of comfort from caring for his grave. I keep the flowers, the grass, and the headstone clean and looking good. We planted a pine tree next to his headstone. His father and I will be buried on one side of him and his grandparents will be on the other side. He is close to his great grandparents and his great-great grandparents. My mother died at my birth at age 22. My father died about 12 years ago. I believe that Matt has met them in the spirit world and that he is with them. I believe that he is not alone and they are loving him and taking care of him for me until I can be with him again. I could not endure the pain without this knowledge. The smell of him eventually left his room and his clothes. I wish it had lingered longer. I still occasionally look for Matt, just as if nothing ever happened and believe I have felt him near at times and that things are okay for him.

I have always had a great sense of peace when it comes to Matthew's spiritual status. I don't believe that his intent was to die. I believe he was physically and emotionally exhausted. Perhaps, he was not rational. And he was only a child. I have pleaded and prayed for answers and this is the answer and peace I continue to receive. I know that our Father is a loving father who judges us much more wisely than we judge ourselves. He, and only He, knew Matt's intent when he took his life. His Father in Heaven loves him more than I love him and, I believe, welcomed him home.

"I was in shock. I couldn't believe my only son was dead."

DAN RAY ADAMS

By Maxine Zawodniak

Dan was an only child of a very unhappy marriage that ended in divorce when he was about eleven. I remarried when he was 12. After a difficult adjustment for 6 months, Dan and his stepfather built a relationship of value. When his stepfather joined The Church of Jesus Christ of Latter-daySaints we were a more united family.

Dan was a good kid, a good teen, and a fine young man. He served a mission, got married in the temple, and promptly divorced. After his divorce, he went to live with his biological father in California. Life there was easy. He could come and go as he pleased with no accountability but he was still a fine young man. He never got into drugs, smoking, or much drinking. His friends were usually students or others he met through acting groups. He was an excellent actor and received many awards at college.

His father died in 1985. A girlfriend moved in with Dan. That lasted a year and a half, then ended very abruptly, and he was devastated again. He went to many counseling groups to help him come to terms with his broken relationships. Two years later he began living with a third young woman. About this time, he became more irritated and agitated. He relied a lot on his girlfriend. After a few months, she left him and he was despondent again. He returned to group therapy and we agreed to pay for a psychiatrist. We told him that this was a time to turn over a new leaf and deal with what was bothering him. He called me often and I went to stay with him for a while. I could see that he was grieving deeply. I didn't know what to say except to give him love and encouragement. At times, I wanted to chastise him for living the way he did and not attending church.

He was going to the psychiatrist once a week and we told him to go more often if he needed it. He was 39 years old at this time. He said the psychiatrist would only give him some light sleeping pills but he always felt better when he talked to him. I asked him to insist on getting an antidepressant.

On Sunday he came to me and told me that he wanted to go see the bishop right then. He wanted to get his life straightened out and get back to church. We went to the bishop's counselor because the bishop was out of town. They talked for over an hour. Dan was very open with him. He received a blessing and President Kimball's book, *The Miracle of Forgiveness*. He also tried to contact the singles organization. He said, "Mom, I promise I am going to get back to church and turn my life around."

I left on Wednesday. I called him when I got home, but there was no answer. I called several times about ten minutes apart. About 1:00 p.m. my phone rang. The voice said, "Maxine, this is Stump [Dan's next-door neighbor]. I didn't want to have to tell you this, but Danny shot himself."

I heard the words. I repeated them in my mind. Finally I said, "Oh no, no!! Dear God, no! What happened?" I was in shock. I couldn't believe my only son was dead. I walked in circles, rubbing my hands, and saying over and over, "Dan is dead! Dan is dead!" But I didn't cry, couldn't cry, did not really believe what I was hearing. Soon the bishop and one of his counselors and my friends came. I just sat there and said, "I don't know why I can't feel."

When John walked in with tears coming down his face, my whole body, especially my chest, tightened up and my voice box closed. It was like a vise was on my voice box and a lead weight was on my chest. It seemed that any minute I would wake up and find that I had been dreaming.

Some of the decisions I made then, I now regret. I was so concerned that I might see some evidence of his gunshot wound, I was afraid to go look right at him or touch him. (He had put the gun in his mouth.) I wish I had touched him. I was sitting really close to him in a chair at the viewing. I was constantly talking to myself: "Look at his hands. They're not stiff, but just lying at his sides. Look at his eyes. Did they glue them? Why did they comb his hair back up over his head? Is that because there was a wound in his head? His hair looks so red. Oh, Baby, you did not have to do that. There is always a way out." I wanted him to know how sorry I was for not helping him more.

Then the questions without answers began. "What if I had never left him?" "What if I had called his doctor and told him to give him the medication?" " What if I had taken over and insisted he just come home with me until he was better?"

We took care of the house in California and disposed of Dan's belongings. After the funeral, Dan's body was sent to Utah to be buried. He was buried on December 20, 1990 on a cold and snowy day. We had a graveside service. I still couldn't believe that my son was in that box. I felt guilty. I reviewed all the times I didn't treat him right, or times I would spank him as a kid, or yell at him. I just knew if I hadn't done that, he would still be here. I reviewed our conversations over the eight days I was there. I kept telling myself, "You knew, you knew this would happen, but you didn't follow through and take charge." The lead weight was still in my chest and I was hoarse. I would cry some and then I would walk the floor. Mostly the pressure inside was unbearable.

Finally I decided if I were going to be able to breathe, I would need a blessing to remove the terrible heaviness from my chest. I called my home teacher, Mike, who was in the bishopric and he gave me a blessing. I didn't know if I totally believed in blessings, but this time I just asked him to have this heaviness removed from me. I left it up to God. Mike told me that God didn't want me to suffer this way, nor did my son. The awful weight lifted from my chest. I was still grieving, but the heaviness and pressure had gone.

I decided that I needed some counseling. The psychologist and my physician prescribed antidepressants. Although I was still walking in fog, it became a little easier to handle each day. I began to eat and sleep, which helped very much. My husband and I drew together. All we had was each other, so we needed to be able to comfort one another.

I searched the scriptures for any information on suicide. I read Elder Bruce R. McConkie's *Mormon Doctrine.* I prayed. I cried to the Lord and explained that it wasn't Dan's fault, but mine and I should be punished instead if there was a punishment. I read every book on near-death experiences I could find. I found much solace in most of them.

People from California who knew Dan, told me "Dan was not himself, and he would not have done this if he had been." When going through Dan's records, I found a psychiatric evaluation dated 18 months before his death. It said that Dan was extremely depressed and his self-esteem was very, very low. He was having trouble then, and no one, not even he, tried to correct it. I think he could cope as long as someone was there to comfort him and ease his financial worries. When Helen, his girlfriend, decided to leave, it was a fatal blow.

Knowing that Heavenly Father is loving and forgiving helped me. I had believed from childhood that anyone who committed suicide was doomed to hell. I couldn't shake this for a long time even though another family we knew had suffered the same thing. They were close friends of a member of the First Presidency. He had told them that their son was not in hell. He made it clear that the Church does not judge suicide victims. He said that we never know the state of mind or the physical problems these people have; God was loving and kind and would take all things into consideration.

I know that Dan was not well. Suicide was out of character for him. After returning from his mission in 1974, he attended BYU. Many nights he sat in his room and cried. I can see now that he carried depression for almost twenty years. I cannot believe that if my child came to me and I knew that he was suffering as Dan did that I would ever reject him. Dan was God's child and I cannot believe God or Jesus would want him to fail. I believe that Dan will be given opportunities to work and advance. He believed in God and Jesus Christ. He was just sick. If a child breaks a leg, we take him to the doctor to set his leg and give him a pain pill. If our brains or emotions are sick, we can have help and medication to alleviate the pain. There should be no stigma against seeking treatment for a mental illness.

I still have moments when I remember talking with Dan the last days of his life, and I cry because I feel that I let him down. Then other days I can look at his picture and feel no pain. Then I feel guilty for feeling nothing. I ask the Lord at times about this, and the thought that comes is, "Didn't I speak peace to your mind?"

God's love for us was manifested in a comforting spiritual experience some months later. A young mother in our ward was terminally ill with cancer and the day before she died I had a strong impression I should go see her. She had been in and out of consciousness. When she awoke, she said: "Oh, Maxine, I prayed you would come. I saw your son Dan. He told me to tell you he was okay but you need to let him go. He said people may be hampered in their progress on the other side when the family will not relinquish their grief." Chastened but comforted, John and I walked to the cemetery that afternoon and told Dan we loved him and missed him but we could let him move on with his life in the spirit world. We were at peace.

I find that I am very compassionate with anyone who has lost a child of any age. I am not nearly as afraid to die or even talk about my death. I don't know if I have grown spiritually or not. I know that there is a God. I know that there is life after death. I know there was life before we came here because I have had the blessing of remembering it. On one occasion, the Prophet Joseph Smith made the following declaration:

> When you climb up a ladder, you must begin at the bottom, and ascend step by step until you arrive at the top; and so it is with the principles of the Gospel--you must begin with the first, and go on until you learn all the principles of exaltation; but it will be a great while after you have passed through the veil before you will have learned them. It is not all to be comprehended in the world; it will be a great work to learn our salvation and exaltation even beyond the grave. *Teachings of the Prophet Joseph Smith*, p. 348 ©2000 Intellectual Reserve Inc.)

UNDERSTANDING THE HEALING PROCESS: DENIAL AND SHOCK

Denial and shock are usually the first reactions in the grieving process. When you first hear of the suicide shock typically occurs. Shock is a form of denial. You may experience shortness of breath, tightness in the throat, a need to sigh, muscular limpness, and loss of appetite. As illustrated in the stories above, the shock wears off, the physical symptoms lose their intensity and the survivor begins to absorb a little more of reality.

Those who have experienced the suicide of a family member have described it as: a "bad dream", "nightmare", "unreal", or "It happens to other people, not me." It is extremely difficult to struggle through the questions that may never be answered in this earth life. Because you are bewildered by what has happened, you search for reasons. Perhaps a suicide note may help interpret what the person was thinking before the suicide. Yet the painful questions remain: "Why did she do it?" "Was he angry with me?"

As discussed earlier, we do have some clues about why people choose suicide. Suicide is often the response to some kind of loss, to real or perceived failure, to physical, psychological, or spiritual pain. The person's problem becomes the only thing that exists, and he or she cannot conceive that life will ever become any better. Part of the healing process is learning to live with unanswered questions. You must gradually let go of the agonizing questions, accept what has happened, and go on living.

Another aspect of denial is the stigma attached to suicide. It is seen by many as something that happens to very dysfunctional or "bad" families. In the LDS culture, some believe that a person who commits suicide will be damned with no hope of salvation. This makes it even more difficult to face the fact that a suicide has occurred. Survivors hope that the medical report was a mistake, that there was an accident, or that the person died of a heart attack. In many cases, there is not enough evidence to resolve the issue completely and the resulting uncertainty prolongs the healing process.

Survivors may avoid discussing the cause of death or actively disguise it. They may feel that denying the suicide will protect the memory of the dead person. Denial is also a way to avoid letting others know that there may have been troubles in the family. To admit suicide took place is to expose personal agonies and failures, imagined or otherwise.

It is common for survivors to want to touch and see the fatal wound or the specific location of the suicide to confirm the reality of their loved one's death.

In a similar way, you may have an overwhelming desire to see your loved one in the casket, to touch the body, to see the wounds. You may go frequently to an empty bedroom just to make sure he or she is not there. Like the mother in the story above, there is a need to see, touch, and feel some things in order to come to terms with reality.

Although a painful phase, denial and shock perform a healthy function. It allows the slow assimilation of loss. It insulates against the jarring impact of suddenly losing someone who has been a significant part of your life. Nevertheless, feelings of denial will eventually pass and you will gradually face reality.

Sometimes friends and family think it is best for you to face reality, now! They want you to accept the fact that your loved has killed himself or herself. They want you to become involved in all of the things you did before the death. They may think that enough time has passed. They love you and it is difficult for them to watch you experience so much pain and suffering that is a part of the grieving process. Recovery of course, is personal and you must decide on your own pace. Take your time accepting reality. Be patient with yourself.

Denial and shock take time to subside. The good news is that tremendous growth and acceptance will come as you accept the truth. Eventually these feelings will pass and you will begin to face the reality of your loss. As you allow time for terrible memories to play their role, the hurt becomes less intense, and good memories begin to surface again.

Remember, out of the darkness and horror of Calvary came the voice of the Lamb, saying, *"Father, into thy hands I commend my spirit."* (Luke 23:46.) The dark was no longer dark, for He was with his Father. He had come from God and to God He had returned.

HELPS FOR THE HEALING PROCESSES:

Confronting denial is an important step of recovery. Answering the following questions has been found helpful to those facing the reality of a suicide. The first question focuses on the individual committing the suicide.

♦ *"It is hard to believe he or she killed himself or herself because . . ."*

A survivor might respond by saying, *"She had problems but life wasn't that bad for her. She had a job . . . "* or *"He couldn't have killed himself. It must have been an accident because . . ."*

♦ The second question is related to the survivors. It is: "I believed it couldn't happen to me and my family because . . ."

A survivor might answer with *"I've been active in the Church my whole life, bad things shouldn't happen to me . . ."* or *"We've been a close family, it could never happen. We love one another . . ."*

List as many responses as possible to these two statements. These questions could be answered privately in writing or by talking with a trusted friend.

Chapter 6

ANGER AND BLAME

"Most of all I felt anger at God"

PFC JAMES V. GARDNER, U.S. Marine Corps

By Arlene Ball,

OBITUARY

PFC James V. Gardner, USMC died October 1, 1991 of a self-inflicted gunshot wound in Silverdale, Washington.

He was born July 9, 1973 to David and Arlene Gardner in Ely, Nevada. His father and a brother, also named David, preceded him in death. He grew up in Cedar City and graduated from Weber Basin High School in 1990. He was a member of the LDS Church and a Life Scout. He entered the Marine Corps in November 1990 and was serving in Marine Security at Bangor Naval Submarine base at the time of his death. He loved the Marine Corps and believed in the ideals it served.

James was a quiet sensitive boy who was dearly loved and he will be missed. He was mischievous and fun loving, but a serious, deep thinker. He loved Christmas, his friends, his mother, and his brother and sisters. Maybe he didn't love himself enough to accept his own imperfections and the unpredictability of life.

While James chose to take his own life, we believe he was received by loving arms on the other side and that our Savior, who feels all our pain, knows and accepts James as the valuable child of God that he is, that his existence still holds validity and purpose.

We as a family ask all families to show each other a little more love today, in honor of our precious son, and cling to life as a gift from God.

James had been dead almost twenty-four hours when two Marines knocked on my door. There were no premonitions, no warnings from the spirit that something was wrong. When I saw the military van drive up and two uniformed men get out, I was talking on the telephone. I felt a slight chill, but dismissed it because I had been expecting someone from the military to contact me for a routine security clearance.

I was cheerful and unsuspecting as I watched them cross the lawn and walk up the steps. I met them at the door with a "Hi" and a smile. That must have made it harder for them. They asked if I was James' mother and I said, "Yes, is he okay?" They didn't answer my question, just asked if they could come in. A stillness came over me and I repeated, "Is my son all right?" Again they replied, "Please ma'am, if you would just let us come in and talk to you." I felt as if someone had hit me in the back of the neck with a board and the shock came in waves. The Marines caught me as I collapsed. They carried me to the couch as I sobbed questions. They explained that he had shot himself. I was shaking so hard and in so much shock that I couldn't tell them my husband's number at work. I could see the soldiers' faces swimming above me, trying to talk to me, tears in their eyes.

They finally reached my husband at work and told him that James was dead. When he came home we sat on the couch and held each other in disbelief. My first husband, (James's father) and an older son, had been killed 18 years before in a drowning accident. Bill and I were married when James was nine, and his two children, Jared and Jessie, were five and three. James, Jared, and Jessie had bonded as siblings. Sarah, now age five, was born to Bill and me later. It never occurred to us to keep James's suicide from the children. When Jessie came home, Bill quietly told her and she began to sob in his arms. We explained to Sarah in as simple a manner as we could that James had chosen to take his own life. We told her that we didn't know why, but that James must have felt very sad inside and that he was with Jesus now. "This is like a huge nightmare," Jared said that night. Despite the shock there was a gentle feeling in our home. We all loved James and there was no feeling of shame or embarrassment.

I couldn't sleep so I went downstairs into James' room and called the Marine Base to see if there had been some mistake. The commanding officer called me back and said no one knew why James had killed himself, there was no note, and no one was aware of any problems.

I began to plan his funeral. At the time of my first husband's funeral I was in deep shock and so inexperienced that the funeral didn't pay adequate tribute to those I'd loved. I didn't go through the necessary grieving rituals. This time I made plans that would allow our children and James' friends and close relatives to honor him and say good-bye in a way that would allow closure for all of us. I wrote his obituary at 2:00 a.m. The words flowed into my head. I didn't try to hide the fact that James had killed himself. To do that would be to disown my son. I wasn't ashamed of him and I wasn't going to act as if I were. It was hard for my husband to accept my honesty and openness, but I knew I was right and insisted that it be printed as I had written it. That proved to be a good decision. It helped us to avoid a lot of questions and enabled our children to deal with it in an honest, open way.

During the next week, as we prepared to bury James, I felt fairly calm and strong, although the pain would hit periodically. I instructed my family and friends not to touch me when I cried because then I felt like I had to stop. It was hard for them but they did as I asked. I think I was guided and strengthened through those awful days, although at the time I felt very alone.

James' girlfriend, Shanna, said she received a letter from him talking about marriage plans. Marriage plans? He had told me he was breaking up with her! A pattern of secrets and inconsistencies began to reveal itself as time went by. It was very confusing, but it demonstrated James' confused frame of mind, his ambivalence and pain.

I discovered other things that James hadn't told me. He'd found tumors on his testicles and feared they might be cancerous. They were benign, but he still feared he'd be sent home. It had been his dream for years to be a Marine. Perhaps it appeared to him as if his dream was ended. He was the last in his group to receive his security clearance because his health exams had delayed it. The day before he died, he'd gotten into a shoving match with another Marine and lost badly. He'd had a hard time dealing with the humiliation. I could only speculate on his frame of mind, but I knew that appearances were very important to him. I felt awful knowing that he'd been so worried and hadn't been able to confide in me. I'd thought things were fine. Regret was and still is my constant companion.

Because James died in the military, there had to be several investigations and an autopsy. His body was flown in on Sunday night, accompanied by two Marines from the base. When we went to the mortuary I asked to see James alone. That body in full Marine dress blues didn't look like my son. But I took off his gloves and knew they were James' hands. I sobbed and held him and asked, "What have you done to yourself? Why did you do this?" I sensed his presence in the room very strongly and I felt that he was in the Savior's care. I stayed in the room for a long time, touching him, trying to warm his hands, talking to him, and crying.

In addition to guilt and bewilderment, I felt angry. Not anger at James, but anger at the military because they had so little explanation and the investigation would take months. ("Months? Months? I won't survive months!" I said, but I have.) Most of all, I felt anger at God. I'd been trying to live a good life. I'd been trying to serve others. I was far from perfect, but I was trying hard and I'd prayed often for James. God knew what it would do to me. Why didn't he protect James? Why didn't he at least give me a chance to say goodbye? I deserved it after burying my husband and other son. I thought he must not love me. People say to me, "God didn't do it, James did." I know that. But does God have a hand in our lives or not? If not, why do we bother to pray? Rebellious thoughts filled my mind during those agonizing days.

We decided not to open the viewing to the public, not because James' face was damaged, but because I felt his family and friends needed more private time to say their goodbyes. That also was a good decision. We gave his loved ones as much time as they needed to be alone with his body. Sarah wanted to see his whole body, so we removed the flag and opened the lid, took off his shoes and let her see and feel his hands and feet. I tried to be very natural about this, while expressing my own shock and sorrow in a way that would allow her to deal with her brother's death as a child, not as my support. She was solemn, but not horrified. I believe this was the proper approach for her. She has been able to cry and question and understand as much as a child can. We talked with our children prior to the funeral and afterwards, discussing the reality of the resurrection and the spirit world. Elder Boyd K. Packer's analogy of the hand and glove was helpful to us. (See "An Apostle Speaks to Children," *Friend*, July 1973)

By the day of the funeral, I was exhausted from planning as well as dealing with visitors. I was trying to be gracious and calm and peaceful. It was a nice funeral, a tribute to the special person James was. My sister's children sang a medley of songs, and at the end her son sang a solo dedicated to me. It was a beautiful song about mothers. All I could feel was a bitter anguish. If I'd been that kind of mother, my son wouldn't have shot himself. King David's lament at the death of his son, Absalom, echoed through my mind: "O my son Absalom, my son, my son Absalom, would God that I had died for thee, O Absalom my son, my son!" (2 Samuel 18:33)" I felt a soul mate in King David.

The Marines provided a military ceremony at the cemetery. It was conducted with all the dignity and majesty they could give, presenting me with the flag and playing Taps. I was grateful for the respect with which they treated my son's body and memory.

During the next few weeks, our lives took on a pattern. In the morning I would cry and in the afternoon I would pull myself together and try to mother my family. I had very little to give anyone emotionally. I still felt so much anger with God that it was hard to pray. I begged God to give me a vision, just to let me talk to James for one minute, to see him, to hear his voice. I finally forced myself to go to the store, feeling as if I were naked before these people who surely knew what a failure we'd been as a family. People were strange, some genuinely kind and caring, expressing their sympathy. Others walked quickly by with a big smile and a "Hi, how are you?"-not waiting for an answer. Some people just don't know what to say. Others didn't even know he was dead. I think that it's up to the survivors to bridge the gap at times like this and make it possible for others to share their feelings with us, rather than holding a grudge. It's impossible for someone who hasn't experienced this type of loss to truly understand. We need to allow ourselves to feel the resentment and hurt, but it's better to give others the benefit of the doubt.

The holidays came soon after James died. Christmas was James' favorite holiday so we built a snowman on his grave and put a small artificial tree there. I felt close to Jesus because I was so certain that James was in his care. Christmas was an opportunity to show my gratitude. (Somehow I felt like I was on speaking terms with Jesus, but not Heavenly Father.)

I held up until after Christmas. I tend to be reclusive, especially if I'm hurt, so I retreated into a shell. This was very hard on my husband, but he tried to be understanding and supportive. It frightened him and the other children when they came home to find me still in my nightgown, hair uncombed, sitting in the television room watching "Geraldo", eating junk food, and sobbing that I had nothing left to live for. I felt so lost, such a failure, and James was so totally gone.

I began to contact other mothers of suicide victims and to take some comfort from their total empathy. I bargained with God, begging him to let me wake up in a morning past, to some point where I could change things, from the time James was a baby until the day he died. I fantasized how I would live each minute over and do it better. All of my mistakes were so clear. I did maintain some perspective, enough to keep living. A lot of people have sad, terrible lives and they don't kill themselves. That thought got me through an hour or two. I struggled with my own desire to die to be with him. I still do. I would never consider suicide now, but I still long to be with him.

While I tortured myself, I shut everyone out except my Sarah. I had little to give, even to her. I went through the motions of going to church. People would say how strong I was. They didn't know the agony I was feeling, the bitterness, or the despair. What a struggle it was just to get up and get dressed in the morning. I read accounts of near death experiences again and again. I wanted to know where James was and what he was doing. I was obsessed. I made plans to fly to Seattle to visit the base where he'd died and see the actual spot--that cold bathroom--where my son breathed his last. I worried how I would appear to his friends. Would they think I made him do it? Would they think he was justified?

I dimly realized during this period that I was losing my mind to grief. My doctor prescribed antidepressants and I began taking them before my trip to Seattle to visit the Marine Base where James died. I was able to remain calm and controlled throughout the visit.

My daughter, Jessie, and James' girlfriend, Shanna, accompanied me. We spent five days in the area. I attended the ward James would have been a member of and arranged to meet with his bishop. I gave him a picture of my son, his obituary, and a funeral program. I told him that James was in his ward and that I didn't blame him or the ward for his suicide or lack of activity, but I didn't want him to die anonymously: "the 18-year-old Marine who committed suicide." The high councilman who spoke that day talked about finding these young servicemen as soon as they arrived on base, making contact, and befriending them.

After I came home from Seattle, my attitude started to change, in part due to the medication, and in part to a new therapist who forced me to deal directly with my feelings. She had me write a letter to James. I wrote eight pages. I read it aloud in his room, I read it aloud on his grave, I read it over and over and felt cleansed of the tiniest part of my pain.

In February, my husband and I attended the temple for the first time since James died. During the session, I meditated on the nature of Heavenly Father. How could he love me and still permit James to take his own life? The thought came to me, "Arlene, you believe in Jesus. You believe that He loves you, that He cares about mankind and that He tells the truth. You must believe Him when He tells you that God is good, that He also loves you." Those words struck me with unusual force and I began to pray from a different point of view from that time on. One week later, my close friend's husband was diagnosed with pancreatic cancer. I agonized over tragedy in my friends' lives, but I also realized that God wasn't picking on me only. I was able to rise above my own grief and try to support and empathize with my friends.

I requested all of James personal effects from the base and the investigation results, including the pictures and videotape taken at the scene of his death and the clothes he was wearing. For some people, this might not be a good decision, but for me it was the right thing to do. I felt like I needed to know everything and see everything in order to make it real and put it behind me. Five years later, there is still some question as to whether James actually did commit suicide. I have joined with other parents across the country to improve the investigative process and make sure the government does everything they can to determine the cause of death in James' and others' cases. I haven't done this to deny the possibility of suicide. I feel in my heart that he did take his life. It seems to be the nature of suicide to leave survivors continually wondering. Having as much information as possible helps remove some of the confusion.

I have made many new friends among the "sorority" of mothers who have lost their children to suicide and I've strengthened my previously existing friendships. They have become more precious to me because they have stood by me in my sorrow.

My children still grieve for James and his loss is felt keenly in our home. My two older children met briefly with a therapist. We are seeking the Lord's help in all of our struggles. We may never reach complete resolution in this life. James' friends and older cousins have also had difficulty dealing with his death. Two of his friends missed so much school in the months following his death that they were unable to graduate with their class. A pervasive sense of sadness has bonded us. We worry about the tendency to view suicide as a viable option when the chips are down.

We still pray for James every day, knowing that he needs our prayers just as much as he ever did. I believe that one of the consequences of his act is to see our suffering. How awful it must be to see your loved ones suffer so and not be able to offer them comfort. However, I believe that God is far more merciful in these circumstances than we can ever comprehend.

The pain of his loss is still with me. I believe it always will be. Sometimes the ache hits me with the sharp clarity of those first few days and I cry aloud with the impact. I think every day about why he did what he did and agonize again over my mistakes that contributed to his decision. I must face these mistakes with brutal honesty in order to heal. I know that there is a fine line between honesty and eternal self-punishment and I am trying to forgive myself. I wanted to be a good mother. I wanted the best for my son. His choice was not my choice.

The worst mistake I made with James was the atmosphere I lived in. I was afraid to let him hurt or suffer or experience fear. I tried to protect him from life and perhaps did not instill within him the courage to try or to fail. As I pray and listen to the spirit, the strongest message I receive is to try to put aside fear, to enjoy life, to trust in the goodness of others, and to expect good from life.

I have spoken several times with Elder Marion D. Hanks, whose generously compassionate spirit and kind words have comforted me immensely. I know that we cannot judge those who commit suicide, but must trust in the loving goodness of God to deal with them in a fair and merciful way. Elder Hanks has a small plaque in his office that expresses the idea: *"To know there is a God is to know that all the rules will be fair and that there will be wonderful surprises."*

I have found a poem that sums up my current attitude. I do not know the author, but I offer it as a message of hope to all who may suffer the same agony I have lived through with my family, and survived.

I thought that time could never reconcile me to my loss,
I thought to the end of living, it would be my cross-
A heavy weight that I would have to carry to the last.
But time was kinder than I thought; grief died, and sorrow passed.
I thought I'd lost forever all my joy in lovely things
Wood and gardens, dawns and sunsets, leaves and waves and butterfly wings.
I never thought my heart would leap to greet a friend once more
And listen to the welcome sound of footsteps at the door.
Once again, within the magic web of life I'm caught
Time, indeed, was kind to me, for time, its healing brought.

Private collection of Karen Posey, deceased.

My prayer is that God will bless all of us in this situation and that time will be kinder than we can now imagine. I pray that we will have the strength to endure with faith in the future and in the eternal goodness of God.

Arlene Ball

"THE BISHOP'S SON"

By "Thomas"

I've gone through a lot of things in my life that were hard to bear; my younger brother was killed in a car accident, my youngest brother died from diabetes at a young age. I also lost a sister and both of my parents, but my son's death was the hardest thing I've ever had to deal with.

Gary was probably my best friend. We spent a lot of time together. When he was little he liked sports and I coached his baseball and basketball games. I loved watching him play. A little later, he learned to bowl and found he had a natural ability for the game. I always went with him to his tournaments and shared his happiness when he won. He won a lot of trophies and our happiness overflowed when he bowled his first 300 game. For this he got a beautiful ring that I sometimes wear to feel that happiness again.

When he was little he went to Primary and scouts, and participated in the Roadshows. (He loved being in the Roadshows) Gary attended a different elementary school than his friends did because of the way the boundaries were drawn. The older he got, the more out of place he felt. He graduated from Primary but then he gradually quit going to Church.

When he went into high school he tried sports and tried to be friends with the others who played, but he never felt included in the activities. One group of students who accepted everyone was the "Parking Lot" crowd. When he found this group, for the first time he felt he had friends. They smoked and drank and did some drugs, but they accepted him. The more he went around with this group the less interest he had in school. He dropped out altogether at age 16. He had several jobs but they didn't last long. He really didn't know what he wanted to do.

When he was about 20, Gary met and married a girl he

loved a lot. For a while they were really happy and he vowed to give up the things that were bringing unhappiness. Life was good. He loved his wife, liked his job and was happy. Then some of his old "friends" started coming round. He started drinking again and his life began to deteriorate. He and his wife divorced and he moved back home. We had always been close, but during this time our relationship deepened. He enrolled at the YCC and completed high school. He got a job he liked and things were good, but he was lonely. He wanted a family of his own. Both of his brothers had families and he was very close to their children. In fact, he was their favorite person. He tried very hard to be someone they could look up to and be proud of. It became harder for him as he wanted children of his own so much.

During this time we spent a lot of time together. When he was working nights, he'd wake me early and say, "Come on, Dad. Let's go for a ride." He'd get coffee and I'd get hot chocolate and we'd just ride around. He loved riding on country roads or in the mountains. It really didn't matter as long as we were together. He decided to make some changes in his life again. He quit smoking entirely and began a body-building program. He looked and felt so much better and actually began to like himself, but he was still lonely. As the loneliness would build, he'd eventually find some of his old friends, usually at a bar. The next day he would feel regret and vow it wouldn't happen again.

The day before he died, we helped with ward clean-up-day. He worked so hard and enjoyed being with the other guys there. He came home, got cleaned up and went to a street festival in Ogden. I didn't hear him come home, but it was late.

The next morning I went to bishop's meeting and then my wife and I attended the other Sunday meetings. It was about 4:00 p.m. when I got home. My wife asked me to go downstairs and get him for dinner. He didn't wake when I called his name. When I turned on the light, I saw him lying back on his pillows and that he had shot himself in the heart. I reached out to hold him but his spirit had gone. Thoughts raced through my mind—with my

Priesthood, I could heal him—if only I was good enough—so I gave him a blessing. I was bishop of our ward at the time. I remembered how Jesus had raised the dead and I wanted so much to have the faith to bring my son back to me. I went to the stairs to tell my wife, I said: "My God, he's dead. Gary's dead!" And I literally felt my heart break.

After that things were pretty much a blur. Our other sons were on vacation so they had to be located. The police came and my wife and I were taken to a neighbor while they removed his body from our home. My counselors in the bishopric, Paul and Allen, did everything possible to make it easier, and there was a great out-pouring of love from the ward members.

I was standing at the foot of his casket when I realized that he was just 33 years old, the same age the Savior was when he died. I had a great feeling of empathy for our Father in Heaven who had watched His Son die on the cross.

In the weeks that followed, Sundays were very hard. It was only the love of the ward members that sustained us.

I never became angry with God, but sometimes I felt angry with Gary for leaving me with such emptiness. We were such good friends and it seemed so unfair. But even that I understand. He just got tired of starting over. Suicide is so hard for me to understand. Many think that those who take their lives are doomed to hell. I don't believe that. I think God is much wiser, kinder, and more loving than we can imagine.

We, as God's children need to open our hearts to those who feel they don't fit in. Gary longed for acceptance by the neighbors and other ward members, but he never felt it. As with so many, the nicest things said about him were said after he died. One of the things that make a suicide so hard is knowing the depth of despair that they must feel. They think it is the only way to find peace. As the parents we always tried to fix things so he could be happy but we had to realize that this time we couldn't fix it. All we can hope is that he has found his peace.

It's been two years now since he died and gradually I am finding ways to cope. There will never be a day or an hour that I don't think of him and miss him. The many kind sets of friends help me so much. A sister who lost a son in much the same way Gary died brought us a picture of the Savior holding a young man in His arms as He welcomed him home. It makes me feel better each time I look at it.

Another friend brought a small birdhouse with tires and tools scattered around and a sign that reads "Gary's Car Repair." She knew of his love for cars. On my desk sits a card with a poem that eases my pain when I read it. We put part of it on his headstone.

> Don't think of him as gone away,
> His journey's just begun.
> Life holds so many facets.
> Earth is only one.
> But think of him as living
> In the hearts of those he touched.
> For nothing loved is ever lost and
> He was loved so much!
>
> --E. Brenneman

UNDERSTANDING THE HEALING PROCESS: ANGER AND BLAME

Of all the stages in the grieving process, anger and blame can be the most difficult for a survivor to understand and for others to accept. Typically, individuals move from the denial stage to the anger stage when they begin to realize that their loved ones' deaths were suicides. Losing someone precious hurts and seems unfair, especially when it would seem to be preventable. Survivors often believe they or someone else should have prevented this loss. There is a tendency to assign blame. Survivors of suicide may feel anger towards the suicide victim, their family, their church leaders, themselves, and often toward God. Anger and blame may also be directed at institutions such as hospitals, a church, the military, the police or the government.

Behaviors associated with the anger phase of grief include blaming, yelling, resentment, and periods of rage and bitterness. Anger can become so intense that it can split families apart, alienate friends, and push the survivor away from God and religious activities. You may think, "I have been a faithful and good person my whole life. Why would God allow this to happen to me?" It is not unusual to question personal religious beliefs in this stage. Beliefs you have taken for granted for years are now closely examined and questioned. Intense loss such as suicide can cause a rational person to become irrational, or a religious person to become confused and turn away from church and friends temporarily.

Because of this roller coaster of emotions during the early stages of grief you, the survivor, may feel yourself becoming very scatterbrained, unorganized, or unable to make simple decisions. In addition, a survivor can expect periods of denial and shock to occur or reoccur.

It is natural and appropriate to explore and acknowledge these feelings of anger and blame, because by doing so you are better able to work through this phase of grief. Instinctively survivors tend to reject the way their loved ones chose to end their lives. You may be angry with the deceased for checking out of the relationship and breaking your heart. Remember anger indicates there has been an investment. We don't get angry with someone we don't care about. So anger is not the opposite of love but a dimension of it—a sign of a love deeply wounded. Recovery from the suicide of a loved one is a monumental task for the process of mending a broken heart is painful and slow.

It is important to know that if someone really wants to die, you can't always stop them with your words, prescribed medication, psychiatric hospitalization, your love or your prayers. Mentally you may realize that, but it will take a while to convince your heart.

Handling anger appropriately can help you survive and reenter life or it can become destructive. It depends on how you channel it. As you allow yourself to feel anger, the hurt usually becomes less intense and good memories will eventually surface. Be aware that persistence of intense anger over a number of years can often be a clue that you may not have resolved the first phase of grief, denial and shock. When anger rages unabated, it is often misdirected anger that cannot be alleviated with the passage of time, because the person is not facing the true source or target of their angry feelings.

The Lord has made it clear what He would have us do with anger: "Behold, this is not my doctrine, to stir up the hearts of men with anger, one against another; but this is my doctrine, that such things should be done away" (3 Nephi 11:29,30) This command from the Lord presupposes agency. It is an appeal to survivors to believe that anger can be removed. Prayer is helpful in eliminating anger.

Ultimately, anger can be healed through a willingness to forgive your loved one and yourself. Although you may not believe it is possible, you'll be able to forgive. Right now the anger and other feelings you are experiencing are probably so intense you may have no desire to consider forgiving yourself, the deceased, God or anyone else. That's typical. It's not easy seeing a loved one take his or her life. Today, you may believe that someone has to be responsible for the suicide, and maybe they are. But your ability to forgive will come as you seek the Lord's spirit in prayer. To forgive is a tremendous burden lifted and typically is done little by little, and with enormous effort. A spirit of forgiveness toward those who may have or seemed to have wronged you is the very essence of the gospel of Jesus Christ. Each of us has need of this spirit.

Hard to do? Of course. The Lord never promised an easy road. Learning to let go of your anger and blame can be very painful. The price is high, but the rewards attained are worth all they cost. During this phase, don't get upset if you have mixed emotions and take "one step forward, two steps back." This is normal. Accept the behaviors of anger and blame as part of the healing process and a sign of change. The Lord himself turned the other cheek, He suffered Himself to be buffeted and beaten without remonstrance; He suffered every indignity and yet spoke no word of condemnation. As He hung on the cross, "Then said Jesus, *Father, forgive them; for they know not what they do.* And they parted his raiment, and cast lots." (Luke 23:34 emphasis added) Yes, eventually you too can forgive them, all of them!

HELPS FOR HEALING

The following ideas have been found helpful to those dealing with anger and blame.

- ◆ Recognize anger when you are experiencing it. Identify those people, institutions or others (including yourself) whom you feel are to blame for your loved one's suicide. A survivor might want to write it down.

♦ Discuss your anger and blame with an understanding friend or talk about it with God. Tell why it is so difficult for you to let it go and forgive.

♦ Share your anger and resentment to the deceased by writing a letter about what they have done to you and your family. Make sure you include how much you'll miss them.

♦ Turning to the Lord in earnest prayer can remove angry, bitter feelings and let the Comforter fill your heart with sweet forgiving.

Chapter 7

GUILT AND BARGAINING

"I needed to work through my feelings of guilt"

LISA

By Marilyn Harris

You never comprehend the reality of suicide or death until it happens. We had tried over a period of months to help our 22 year-old daughter, Lisa. She was married with two children, born 13 months apart, and then had double hernia surgery. Her husband was young and faced challenges neither he, nor we, had encountered before. I cared for Lisa after her surgery in November and then left to help her sister who was having surgery. Soon there were signs that Lisa was having a mental breakdown. She ran away twice. After fasting and prayer we found her, brought her home and tried to help her work through her problems. She was unhappy and wanted a divorce. She started to escape into fantasy and became manic-depressive. Until then Lisa was one of the most Christ-like people I ever knew.

We took her to several counselors, who experimented with one medicine after another. She was hospitalized for a while but nothing healed her completely. One day she drove a car until she ran out of gas somewhere in Nevada. Two truckers picked her up and dropped her at the doorstep of a church in Reno. The minister didn't know who she was. She called herself "Rainbow" which was her Girl Scout name. He took her to a Christian woman who cared for runaway or orphan children. After a few days, she won Lisa's confidence and found out who she was. We were fasting and praying continually asking the Lord to help us find her. When the woman called us, we immediately drove to Reno to get her. She was highly manic and we didn't realize what we were dealing with. Before leaving Reno, we stopped at a restaurant to eat. She wanted to buy something in an adjacent drugstore and I went with her. She tried to get away from me and when I held on to her and asked her to please go back to the restaurant with me, she began to scream and tell the people in the store that I was trying to abduct her. The people didn't know whom to believe. I was so frightened, realizing how sick she was. I prayed and said to one of the men, "Please go into the restaurant and get my husband. My daughter has had a mental breakdown and we're just trying to take her back home." He got Robert and we got her into the car. On the way home, she wanted to stop and get a breath of fresh air. She began to run away into the desert and Robert had to chase her and bring her back.

After returning home, she went into her room, emptied her drawers and dumped all her clothes into the middle of the room and sprinkled bath powder all over to "get rid of the evil spirits." Robert gave her a blessing but we knew she needed hospitalization immediately. Lisa escaped from the hospital, and went to Los Angeles. We could do nothing at first because she was an adult and married. I finally got authority to go get her and they handcuffed her to me during the plane ride home.

A psychiatrist put her on Lithium, which helped her for a little while. The doctor said there were no major side effects. Another doctor told me the week after she died that someone in her condition should never have been self-administering Lithium.

Adding to her stress were the threats of her husband to take her children away from her. Her children were her life. She adored them and felt that the only way she could have them was to stay married. He didn't have enough long-range vision to realize that she needed to be safe for a while and get well and then they could work on their relationship.

The day she died Robert and I were debating who should go to the funeral of a close friend and who should stay home with Lisa. The doctor said Lisa had tried to overdose on Lithium and we should keep an eye on her. Her husband said he would like to take her for a ride with the children. I made him promise he would not let her out of his sight. When we returned from the funeral no one was home. Soon her husband came back with the children and she wasn't with them. He had gone to the store to get milk and Lisa talked him into leaving her alone. I was sick to my stomach as we began looking for her. I sat on the front porch and said: "Robert we've lost her. Now she's gone."

Robert found her downstairs in a room where his collection of antique guns were kept. She had shot herself in the heart. My other daughter began to scream at Lisa's husband, saying, "This is your fault, it is your fault!" And I just said. " No! We cannot deal with it that way. The only way we will get through this is with love." Lisa's husband has carried a terrible burden of guilt because of it ever since. We harbor no anger or bitterness toward him because we realize he didn't understand how ill she was. He has now remarried and has other children. We have a loving relationship with him and his present wife and all their children.

Someone said that suicide is the ultimate revenge. Believing that false idea makes you feel so guilty, so worthless and such a terrible parent. People also say that a suicide victim will never go to the celestial kingdom. Because of personal revelation, I know that statement is not true. The month or so after Lisa died, I was so exhausted physically and emotionally, I stayed in bed. It was as if the Lord sat with me for almost three hours and took me step after step through her experience. I could see that all the doors had closed for her. There are many reasons for suicide but I know in Lisa's case it wasn't revenge, it was absolute hopelessness. She felt that she was all alone. She knew she was not normal and that is what frightened her so. To have her children taken away with no hope of being with them was the major door that closed. It was more than she could bear.

Lisa was very artistic and when we went down to choose her casket, her siblings started laughing and said, "Oh, if we put Lisa in that odd casket, she would come back to haunt us." Several people thought their behavior was irreverent and disrespectful. I thought it was good that the children could laugh and have some relief from the overwhelming tragedy.

Lisa was buried in her temple clothing. At her funeral I received an assurance from the Lord's Spirit of her well-being and that she was now in His loving care. Lisa's children and her brothers and sisters have received similar special assurances from the Lord. Since she died I have felt her spirit close in little personal ways.

Because of my experience with Lisa, I have learned to search out and talk to people who are depressed or suicidal. I have been able to help them find a different perspective. I think they are people Lisa would have wanted me to help. Suicide has been compared to an emotional car-wreck that affects each member of the family differently. Some realize the loss immediately and can give voice to their grief. To others reality doesn't set in until much later. They may not be able to cry or mourn in usual ways. Comfort or help needs to be given on an individual basis.

We took classes at UAMI, which is the Utah Alliance for the Mentally Ill, a support group for families of those who have brain disorders. We learned many significant things. It was helpful to me to have doctors and practitioners at UAMI acknowledge that there are so many things we don't know. Fifteen years ago few people understood brain disorders and doctors wrote admitting they were just as much at a loss for knowing what to do as we were. Most of what we have learned about brain function has been in the last fifteen years.

I needed to work through my feelings of guilt and come to grips with the fact that I wasn't perfect. I know I made mistakes raising our children, but we all do. I did the best I knew how at the time. I also learned how important the human touch is. Even after our children are grown they need our gentle and caring touch. I would say to my children, "Your mother needs a hug." Now they are in their 30's but they still expect a hug before leaving our home after a visit. The physical reassurance of our love is very important to all children.

I learned to be a psychodrama instructor because I wanted to understand the issues and how to be more effective in helping people, especially two of our sons. Many young people who have brain disorders try to self-medicate with drugs, alcohol or tobacco. They use these easily available drugs to relieve their terrible anxiety and emotional pain. When the effects of the drug end, they can go into deeper depression. When one person in the family commits suicide others may be at risk also. When one of my sons threatened suicide several times, I finally said: "Look if you decide to do it, I would be really sad, I would be heartbroken. But I have learned one thing, that if you decide to do it, I can't stop you. But you need to learn to live your life on this side of the veil. You can wake up on the other side with the very same problems, so you might as well stay here and learn how to work through them with people who care about you. We love you and will do everything we can to help you." Robert and I now work with our son when he has an episode. I spend a lot of time with him, listening, talking and assuring him of our love and support. Nutritional foods, vitamins and herbs have also helped our son stabilize, without bad side effects. He is doing very well now. Robert also gives our children blessings. If we love our children, and help them deal with their emotions, their fears and their depressions, they can often learn to handle their challenges.

Criticism or faultfinding is very destructive to a mentally ill person. My husband, Robert, was always so kind to Lisa and was never judgmental. Lisa had endured unkind and critical remarks from some people. We don't realize how damaging and hurtful our negative words can be, even when we mean well. To those who are already emotionally struggling, it can be magnified with devastating results.

What enabled me to survive? I always pray to love others and not judge them, to have my heart open. I go to my scriptures and pray a lot. Turning to the Lord when I felt like I couldn't make it brought me peace and strength. I have an abiding faith in the Lord. I know that the Lord is not punitive but very loving, and He cares for each one of His children. He loves all his children and will be there for them if they seek Him.

I believe we have a kind of fairy tale in the Church that if you do what's right you will live "happily ever after." As I look back over my life in the Church, I have tried my best to do everything right and keep all the commandments, but I have a daughter and two sons who have struggled with bipolar disorders. The Lord gave this scripture to me to help me understand why I had these struggles in my life: "Except a corn of wheat fall into the ground and die, it abideth alone: but if it die it bringeth forth much *fruit."* (John 12:24). With few exceptions, all people will experience the death of a loved one. Whether we grow from the experience and become fruitful in our ability to serve and help others is the challenge. I have been able to help others because I have an understanding of suicide.

Another thing I have learned is the place of pain and suffering in the eternal scheme. The Law of the Telestial Kingdom is "eat, drink and be merry." The Law of the Terrestrial Kingdom is the "Law of the Harvest", or "as you sow, so shall you reap." The Law of the Celestial Kingdom is to walk the path of Christ, the low road of pain and suffering. John Taylor, in a talk (June 18, 1883) said that it was necessary for us to pass through certain ordeals and to be tried. "I heard the Prophet Joseph say, in speaking to the Twelve on one occasion: 'You will have all kinds of trials to pass through. And it is quite as necessary for you to be tried as it was for Abraham and other men of God, and (said he) God will feel after you, and He will take hold of you and *wrench your very heart strings*, and if you cannot stand it you will not be fit for an inheritance, in the Celestial Kingdom of God.'" (John Taylor, *Journal of Discourses* 24: 197 Italics added © Intellectual Reserve Inc.)

How could we expect to become like God and succor those in need of succoring if we have never suffered the pain, the contradictions, and the paradoxes of mortality? The Savior "suffered greater sufferings, and was exposed to more powerful contradictions than any man can be." (Joseph Smith *Lectures on Faith,* Lecture #5, p.48. © Intellectual Reserve Inc.) Through these difficult experiences we learn compassion and understanding. If everything were easy we would never know how to "lift up the hands that hang down and strengthen the feeble knees." (D&C 81:5) The gift of wisdom is bought with the coin of pain and suffering.

I used to think when the Savior said not to judge that it was a nice suggestion, but now I know it is a very deep and serious commandment. We don't know what challenges people are dealing with and we don't have the right to judge. I love Robert because he never once lost the sight of that principle with Lisa. He tries to see the big picture, the eternal perspective. I have had a great soul-stretching experience in life learning not to cast any stones and how to love in a divine way.

"I suffer the pains of guilt"

NATHAN TOOMEY

By Laura Toomey,

On February 24, 1997, our 17 year-old son, Nathan committed suicide. That fact can never be changed. We will never again be able to hold him in our arms and feel his breath on our neck. We will never be able to tell him we love him, and hear those words spoken to us.

Since my son's death, I have had many people tell me, "Laura, I don't know how you do it." I tell them, "You take one day at a time. If that doesn't work, then you take one hour at a time." What they don't know is that many hours have been spent in bed crying, surrounded with wet pillows and pictures of my child. I suffer the pains of guilt . . . if I had only said this . . . or if I had only done that . . .then maybe my child would still be alive. When I had to force myself to get out of bed before noon, I felt I was slipping into depression. Then I stopped to think... "Is this what Nathan felt?" Was he trying to convince himself to take one day at a time, one more hour of survival in the dark pit his mind was falling into?

Nathan was a "typical" teenage boy. He loved to hike, swim in a lake, be with his friends, and he found great joy in laughter. Nathan was known as a very giving person. He literally would give you the shirt off his back if he saw the need. It was not uncommon to hear someone, say..."Yes, it was Nathan who helped me with that." That is why his suicide came as a shock to everyone.

In December of his senior year, Nathan announced to us that he had decided to join the military, as a means to get further education. Within a few weeks, he had narrowed it down to the Marines. He was excited about his decision, and would go around the house singing, "The few . . .the proud . . .the Marines." He took the oath and was scheduled to leave for boot camp as soon as he finished his senior year.

In January, his cousin, Richard, asked Nathan to pick him up at the airport, and drive him to the Missionary Training Center in Provo. It was at this time that we began to see a change in Nathan. He had often talked about going on a mission for our church, and had been preparing himself for this goal. The next part of Nathan's life, we call "his six week shut down period." He went from a happy teenager to a child we could not get out of bed. We would find him in a dark room, just staring at the wall. He stopped eating and taking care of himself. We were not allowed to turn on the lights or make any noise. Unknown to everyone round us, our family was "walking on egg shells."

Ten days before the tragic day, the children had gone to school, Dad had just left for a business trip to California. About 1:00 p.m., I went downstairs to check on Nathan. He had not come upstairs all morning. I found him lying in bed staring at the wall in a dark room. I begged him to go with me to get some lunch, anything to get him out of the house and into fresh air. After no response, I went upstairs and called a family crisis hotline. The counselor told me to get Nathan immediately to a hospital. We called 911 and he was admitted to the psychiatric ward. Less than 48 hours later, due to a mistake concerning our insurance, Nathan was sent back home. He had been diagnosed with bipolar mood disorder.

Monday at 6:40 a.m., at my scream the family came running downstairs to Nathan's room, where he lay lifeless. He had taken over 100 sleeping pills, which he had purchased over the counter at a local supermarket. Only our daughter was spared the horrible image. Her bedroom was upstairs next to ours. She heard Nathan's voice tell her, "Julianne, stay in your room. Do not go downstairs." We immediately called 911 and the home was filled with policemen. We huddled together, sobbing, heartbroken and in shock. There was a note, letting us know of his love for his family. He said he wanted answers to everything, spiritual and earthly. He felt his grandpa would comfort him in heaven, and he said not to ruin our lives by mourning him.

Our bishop and the Relief Society sisters came and took over, intercepting calls and handling many of the details that attended his death. Even though we were fairly new in the ward, the members cleaned our home, prepared food, and helped with the details of the funeral. They wrapped their arms around us with love. What a comfort their compassionate service was.

My husband and I gathered our four children and drove to his parents' home. They were away on a trip, so we could mourn in peace. As my husband and I knelt in prayer at the side of the bed pouring out our sorrow to our Father in Heaven, a very peaceful feeling filled the room. We felt Nathan was there with his arms around us weeping with us. He seemed to speak to us in our minds. He expressed his deep love for his family. He was sorry for bringing us pain. He indicated that he wanted to have baskets and boxes of oranges instead of flowers at his funeral. We asked for the oranges and they came by the boxful.

Suicide is a very selfish act. It leaves a grieving family and friends who will feel the loss of a loved one forever. The "whys" and "if onlys" cause family members to feel guilt and pain. Knowing that many teenagers would be at the funeral, I asked our bishop to talk about suicide. He said it was the hardest talk he ever had to give. The bishop quoted from an article in the October 1987 Ensign in which Elder M. Russell Ballard explained that suicide is a sin, yet the Lord will not judge the act alone, but He will look at that person's circumstances and the degree of accountability.

Elder Ballard then quoted from Elder Bruce R. McConkie:

"Persons subject to great stresses may lose control of themselves and become mentally clouded to the point that they are no longer accountable for their acts. Such are not to be condemned for taking their own lives. It should also be remembered that judgment is the Lord's; He knows the thoughts, intents, and abilities of men; and He in his infinite wisdom will make all things right in due course." (Elder M. Russell Ballard, *Ensign*, October, 1987, p. 7 © 1987 Intellectual Reserve Inc. used by permission)

At the conclusion of the funeral, we showed a slide presentation of Nathan's life, which left everyone in tears. Then, as difficult as it was, my husband Dave and I felt impressed to speak. Dave spoke of his concern for the youth suffering depression and how quickly a tragedy may occur. He talked directly to the high school students present and told them suicide should never be considered as an answer for their problems. He encouraged students to seek help from the many sources available that can help them deal with their difficulties. I told the audience I had craved oranges while I was pregnant with Nathan and oranges were his favorite fruit. He wanted everyone who came to the funeral to take home an orange in remembrance of him. He hoped they would think of the sweetness of their friendship with him. Nathan was such a giving person, always willing to help others. His life had meaning and we hoped the orange would remind them of all the good things Nathan did in his short life.

The next few months were very hard. Our children were showing signs of trauma because of seeing their brother lying dead on the floor. One son held his hand on his chest every time he passed Nathan's room, because he felt his heart would explode. Each of us had to fight the image in our minds and we were all put on medication.

Our family has been blessed in many different ways. After Nathan's death, we discovered that he had been keeping a journal for several years. In an entry dated January 31, 1993, Nathan wrote, "I know that I have less than 5 years to live. Let me tell you about myself." He talked about what he liked, and then bore testimony of his belief in Jesus Christ. He quoted his favorite scripture, 3 Nephi 13:6. He wrote about reading the Book of

Mormon: "I was so excited! All my hard work paid off. I had a warm fuzzy feeling, and I could now say that I have read the Book of Mormon." Nathan went on to say: "I testify to you, keep the commandments and be righteous. I know that our Heavenly Father lives and I, too, am a Child of God. The last days are coming soon and I hope that I am saved in the last days. It is very hard for our generation to be faithful. I know I am not perfect and I hope God will forgive me for my sins so I can dwell with Him and speak with Him in the Celestial Kingdom. I say these things with all my heart."

We have recently moved to a new home so that we can start a fresh life. We continue our healing process on a daily basis. We talk about Nathan a lot. One child is afraid that we will "forget" Nathan. No way! In fact, we keep him alive in a humorous way. Whenever someone says "Who didn't flush the toilet?" or "Who didn't shut the door?"...We all say "Nathan", and we laugh. It relieves some of the tension and sadness, because Nathan is still part of our family. He is just temporarily gone. We hope that he can serve a mission on the other side. We know that we will once again hold him in our arms, and feel his breath on our necks.

We feel an inner peace now that he is okay. We have the comfort of knowing that our Savior loves us, and He loves Nathan. We know that our Savior has felt the sorrow we are now feeling. We know that through our Savior's Atonement, we may repent and strive to live the best we possibly can. Most importantly, we know that our family is sealed together forever, and nothing can break that chain.

This experience and trial has brought our family closer together. Our children show a deeper love and respect for their parents and each other. We express that love and appreciation for one another more consistently. We feel fortunate that we have not drifted apart. We are grateful to our Father in Heaven for each new day. We thank Him for the little miracles in our lives that confirm Nathan is okay.

Many times we have felt Nathan near us, still a part of us. One son had a special dream. He and Nathan were sitting on his bed, with their legs dangling over the edge. He talked to Nathan about a problem that he was having. Nathan gave him advice and assured him that everything was going to be all right.

Where do I go to find comfort? First, to my Father in Heaven for he literally carried us through that rough time. I remind myself that Nathan is His son; that I was given the wonderful privilege of caring for, teaching and loving Nathan for 17 years. Second, I find comfort in talking with those who face depression, or know someone they love who is going through it. A simple hug or smile can make a big difference in someone else's life. Try it.

After a discussion with the family, we have decided to sign our names to our message.

Nathan, we love you!

Dave and Laura Toomey
David, Jr., Matthew, Jeremy and Julianne

UNDERSTANDING THE HEALING PROCESS:
GUILT AND BARGAINING.

Several of these accounts including those above, illustrate aspects of the guilt and bargaining phase of healing. When anger begins to subside, you may feel guilty for many reasons. You may think that if you had somehow been more aware, more loving, more controlling, you could have prevented the suicide. You may then ask God to give you another chance, take you instead, or even bring your loved one back. You may also want to bargain with God and plead to Him with promises of "I will read my scriptures more faithfully; I'll be more thoughtful of others; I'll serve more diligently if you will just give me one more chance." Tearfully and in desperation you may beg God to "Let me talk to my loved one; let me see him or hear her voice just one more time."

As you go through this phase of grief, remember that you are human and there are events that you cannot control. Remember that love alone may not be enough to save another's life and that you were not the only influence in the life of your loved one. Guilt feelings are normal because of our powerlessness and imperfections. You may blame yourself for the loss of your loved one for what you did or did not do. At times the individual committing suicide may even leave a note or make comments accusing you of behavior that "caused" the death. After the suicide these feelings of guilt tend to be magnified and can be overwhelming, making life very difficult. Others may actually say or hint that the death may have been your fault. So, ask yourself the question, "Did you have anything to do with your loved one's unhappiness?" You may answer "Perhaps." But your words and behavior could not kill anyone. Your behavior did not make anyone overdose. You did not make anyone feel the feelings or think the thoughts that made suicide an acceptable alternative.

Most people have occasions in which they are unhappy and experience problems. However, most people don't kill themselves as a result. Some do. Many of you reading this book have tortured yourselves with the possibility that you could/should have done something differently, thereby preventing the suicide. Although hospitalization or another form of treatment *might* have helped, no one can be sure that any particular treatment would have saved your loved one's life. Perhaps the suicide might have been averted for a time or even altogether, but there is no way of knowing for sure. None of us knows everything about the "why" and "how comes" of a suicide. We can speculate. We can guess. But, some things only God knows. Some events in life are just mysteries.

Occasionally a survivor can have mixed feelings about a loved one's suicide. Perhaps the one committing suicide had been the source of much conflict and problems in the family. Perhaps you had the thought that things would be better if she or he were gone, or even dead. At times a suicidal person may threaten over and over again, "I'm going to kill myself." After many threats you may have felt like saying, "Why don't you then?" And then they do. You would naturally be devastated by guilt. Relationships can be very stressful and even confusing. One of our most difficult challenges in life is to deal with the agency and choices of others, especially members of our family. You are not responsible for the choice made by your loved one. Any mistakes you made in your family relationships are not sufficient to cause the suicide.

> Elder Neal A. Maxwell said:
> "God leaves us free. He is deeply committed to our moral agency and to letting people make mistakes if they choose to. And war is the reflection of how institutions fail and of the corruption of individuals. And yet, God leaves us mortals free to make decisions. Sometimes God intervenes as in the Noachian flood, or in Sodom and Gomorrah, but not always. And so needless and terrible tragedies occur because of leaders' and people's misuse of their freedom. " *(The Neal Maxwell Quote Book,* "Agency", p.11 Bookcraft, 1997, ed. By Cory H. Maxwell)

Elder Maxwell also gave comfort to us "would-be Saints" who struggle, when he said: "We should allow for the agency of others (including our children) before we assess our adequacy. Often our deliberate best is less effectual because of someone else's worst." *(The Neal Maxwell Quote Book,* "Agency" p. 11 ibid)

At times, your family and friends may try to brush your feelings of guilt aside. Be patient with them. They too, can be overwhelmed with powerful emotions when suicide occurs. Guilt feelings may torment you during the early months of healing. Guilt and bargaining are an attempt to gain control over a situation that you cannot control that can prevent you from facing reality. Guilty thoughts or feelings can paralyze and demoralize you and prolong the healing process.

In the end, you will realize that you are not to blame. You can go on with your life. The road to recovery requires you to accept your feelings and to draw strength from the resources available to you such as prayer, priesthood blessings, scripture study and the love of friends and family.

HELPS FOR HEALING

Of all the emotions associated with suicide, personal guilt seems to be the most intense and painful. Some survivors have found help by performing the following tasks:

♦ Acknowledge the behaviors you, your family, and others were doing before the suicide that were positive and meant to be helpful. For example, a survivor might recall, "I was attending church, praying and trying to do what was right. I tried to talk to the deceased and encourage him or her..." Make a list of all the things you did that were loving and helpful. Most survivors were doing their best given the information they had prior to the suicide.

♦ Assuming the deceased had agency, brainstorm solutions that were available to the deceased that could have been used instead of suicide. The survivor might respond with statements like, "He could have called his counselor. She could have talked to me or to . . ." Of the available alternatives she or he still chose the option of death. These questions could be answered privately in writing or by talking with a trusted friend.

♦ Make it a matter of prayer, fasting and scripture study, asking the Lord to help you see the truth and be released from the burden of guilt.

Chapter 8

DEPRESSION AND LONELINESS

DEPRESSION – A CAUSE AND AN EFFECT OF SUICIDE

"CORY"

By "Shirley"

Our handsome, gifted son "Cory" was born March 23, 1965. He always had a curious mind, even teaching himself to read. He devoured books, was a good athlete, had a strong spirit of competition, and a fun sense of humor. He was always on the honor roll in junior high and high school. He served a mission to Central America. While at the MTC, he became so fluent in Spanish, he was sent to his mission early. He worked with many native companions. It was a challenging mission, but Cory's attitude throughout was positive. He served an honorable mission, and learned to love the humble poverty-stricken people.

Cory returned from his mission in February 1986. He had no emotional problems on his mission, but in March we started to notice symptoms of depression and anxiety. He was experiencing sleepless nights and obsessive, self-devastating thoughts. It was Cory's first experience with severe depression. As my husband, Don, and I watched him become more agitated and disturbed, we obtained psychiatric help for him. Don is a social worker. I took him to the psychiatrist who had been following my case at a university mood disorders clinic. My worst fears were confirmed. The doctor suspected that Cory was a victim of the same mental illness I have--bipolar disorder. He immediately put Cory on medication. To be on medication for emotional problems was difficult for Cory, as it is for many people. He would say, "I don't want to be a <u>druggie</u>! I should be able to handle this myself!" When Cory became more agitated, he would hide his pills or not be consistent in taking them. This only made things worse as it is crucial to stay on consistent prescription dosages.

Cory was on a full academic scholarship at BYU. Even suffering from depression, he was still able to get A's in advanced calculus and advanced Spanish during spring semester, maintaining his 4.0 GPA. When I pointed this out, he retorted, "All I can be is a student! What good is that? I have no other talents!" He was constantly comparing himself with others–especially his brothers who were working. He felt their jobs were much more prestigious than his. Cory was a bagger at a local grocery store. He felt humiliated that he had not advanced to a checker. After all, he was "a returned missionary with over a year's college training" who was working as a bagger with high school students! He had some panic attacks at work. Finally he could not face going to work. He quit, which increased his negative feelings about himself.

I experienced my first bout with depression when I was nineteen. Several years later I was diagnosed with bipolar disorder when I had my first manic attack. The disease often manifests itself in late adolescence and young adulthood. It is a biochemical, genetic illness I probably inherited from my paternal great-grandfather. He suffered "melancholia" (depression) and several descendants have taken their lives.

Just before Cory came home from his mission, I had been tormented with my ninth, four-month long severe depression. I did not want him to come home and find me in this agitated state. For me depression is like a smothering, all-encompassing darkness— being plunged into a bottomless abyss where blackness descends over my entire body, where no light penetrates. Almost miraculously, with a change in medication, the depression lifted just three days before his return. Now in my positive high, I was excited and delighted to welcome him home. Nothing had changed in my physical world. It was a shifting of chemicals in my brain, which to me defies understanding. When my depression lifts, it is like a rebirth for me. I have such a renewed appreciation for the Lord, life, my husband, my family and friends. My previously "black world" becomes beautiful again. I have increased energy, enthusiasm, and sometimes exaggerated euphoria. Then I must guard against the manic dimension of my illness. I must watch that I do not get too high emotionally, that I do not become manic-psychotic, a state which has twice required my hospitalization. In my first psychotic manic episode I was so bad the hospital personnel thought I had taken LSD.

I feel anguish knowing that I have attempted suicide. I know the distortion, the irrationality, and the feeling that my family and friends would be better off without me. On our fifth wedding anniversary, I asked "Don" for a divorce. I was certain he and our two young boys would be better off without me. Because he did not understand the illness as well at that time it was a terrifying, painful time for him. But it has been Don who has helped me the most to be able to "hang on." He would say, "We have been through this before; we will get through it again. *I am here*! There is nothing more important than the two of us, than our relationship."

Paradoxically, with Cory in depression, I learned what it was like to be the well person--the caregiver--trying to convince our depressed son of his self worth and not being able to do so. It had been so recent since my last depression that I still remembered the irrational, negative thoughts and self-comparisons. Admiration for my husband's long-term patience increased. I felt I would always be inferior, never be able to measure up to others. When friends or family pointed out my strengths, I wouldn't believe them. I felt I alone knew the "real truth" about myself. I felt I could not endure this hideous disease one more time. I felt abandoned. My sister wisely said. "You compare yourself with others at their best when you are at your worst." Prayers for help or comfort seemed unanswered. To escape the excruciating painful thoughts I would find refuge by staying in bed, by hiding. Then terrible guilt would follow because I had not accomplished anything! Don tried to help me understand what has become known as the Depressive Triad, described as the following distorted thinking: 1. I am basically defective. 2. I contaminate my environment and the people around me. 3. The negative will never change, and the way I feel now is the way I will feel forever. This is terminology used by professionals in treating depression.

Cory had similar obsessive, self-negative thoughts. I would say to him, "Cory, these bad feelings will not last. What you are thinking is not true. Hang on! Your mood will change. You won't feel this way forever." Yet, in my heart, I knew the depressed person believes a depression will never end! He shot himself September 3, 1986, six months after his return from his mission. I was alone when I found him.

Two days earlier Cory had made a suicide attempt by overdosing on medications. I wanted him hospitalized. Both the doctor and my husband, who is a social worker, felt that to admit Cory would only create more guilt. The day before he died, Cory had been very remorseful, distraught, and tearful. I took him to our family cabin, and we put a difficult puzzle together. I kept trying to keep him distracted.

That night our family had planned to attend a musical. He said he could not go! It was an effort for Cory but he came. The next morning, his mood had improved. He said, "You know, Mom, I think I could take a reduced load at school and still keep my scholarship." I had to remind him that we had withdrawn him from BYU two days before, at the doctor's advice. He looked at me with his penetrating gaze and a look that seemed to say, "So now, I can't even be a student." This was the last time I saw Cory alive.

I was doing household chores. After a time, I went downstairs to check on him. In an instant I saw the small revolver by his outstretched hand. He had shot himself in the right temple. I ran to the phone and dialed 911. An ambulance came quickly, followed by neighbors and friends. I think deep down I knew Cory was dead, but when the paramedics said he was gone, I started screaming hysterically, "No, no, my brilliant son is dead. I knew how sick he was, but no one would listen . . . no one would listen!"

My husband had gone fishing early that morning and came home to find an ambulance and police cars in front of our home, and the house was filled with people. His first comment was, "What a waste!" Don's anguish was intense. When our friends saw us, it was Don for whom they were most concerned. I was definitely sustained that day. When people came to our home, I was often the one able to comfort them.

Later in the afternoon, I went back to Cory's bedroom. All reminders of what had happened had been removed. I knelt by his bed and pled to the Lord for comfort. I received a strong impression that when Cory's special but disturbed spirit left his body, he was received with forgiveness, love, and compassion into the arms of our Savior. The next few days we survived the funeral and the burial because we felt the presence of the Holy Ghost sustaining and comforting us. The love and compassion shown to our family were overwhelming. Perhaps this is what "suffering" is all about--people dropping barriers and trying to comfort, love, and help one another. More than ever before, gospel principles strengthened me. To believe in a life hereafter and a reunion with our loved ones was crucial to my faith.

I had to accept there was no way to change what had happened. I learned, when I got on my knees and would plead for His comfort, the Lord never failed me. During one long and excruciating period of depression a dear friend had told me, "You will not be able to believe me now. But when your depression lifts, you will have a greater compassion for the Savior and his atoning sacrifice in Gethsemane where he descended below all human suffering. He knows and understands your suffering!"

Suicide is a horrific tragedy for everyone. You find yourself saying, "what if" or "I should have" and think about "what might have been." It is so difficult for people who have not experienced severe depression themselves, or seen it in a family member or friend, to really understand how people can be so desperate that they would take their life.

Several weeks after the funeral, a young woman who had fallen in love with Cory after his return, came to see me. She said she had seen Cory in a dream. He was dressed in white and he told her that he was "all right and he was with God." She wanted us to know that he was at peace. This was comforting to me, but I longed for him to appear to me in a dream.

At the funeral family and friends expressed their love and admiration for Cory, and their faith that he was with his Father in Heaven. In his sermon one of our dearest friends spoke these words of comfort and peace:

> A little four-year-old boy ran into his house one day and said, 'Dad, come outside and see what's out there!' The father went outside, looked down at a puddle of water, and the little boy said, 'Dad what is it?' The father said, 'It's just oil that dripped on the water.' The little boy, seeing all the glorious colors spreading out across the water, said, 'Oh . . . I thought it was a dead rainbow.'

> That story has sustained me through the years. It has become my metaphor to describe my relationship to my Father in Heaven. Given what the child knew about death and about rainbows, his answer made good sense. In the same way, with our limited understanding, we try to make sense of the things that happen to us in this world. Our answer, our explanation of things, would probably seem just as limited as the little boy's, if we had eternal perspective.

> But the little boy trusted his father's explanation even though he had no way to know for sure that it was right. That trust is the leap of faith we make in the same way when we trust that Father understands the things we do not. We should not use the word 'waste' when we speak of Cory's life. Who are we to judge the quality of a life by the length of it? Cory's life has been full of excellence, beauty,

accomplishment, laughter, joy and goodness. He fulfilled a fine mission. And then–from my point of view–he got sick and died.

We often wonder why such suffering must exist in this mortal life. But out of pain often comes a finer spirit. Some better self seems to rise up out of us. As we are touched by that fineness of spirit, we want to do what's right. We want to help others. We want to be tender and kind and loving.

Suffering moves us in another way. In Moroni 7:42-43, we read, 'Wherefore, if a man have faith, he must needs have hope, for without faith there cannot be any hope. And again, behold I say unto you, that he cannot have faith and hope, save he shall be meek and lowly of heart.' It is in our lowliness of spirit and meekness in times of grief, or in times of challenge—that we feel faith, and out of faith comes hope. Of course, that hope which we all share is hope that death is a temporary separation– and we start to get some perspective.

Don and Shirley are celebrating their twenty-fifth wedding anniversary today, the day of their son's funeral. A cynic might call that a terrible, fatalistic irony. I find it poignant. Shirley's life has been one of the greatest examples of courage that I know. She never gives any indication of the pain and anguish of depression that she has had to live with most of her life. She does not view her life as tragic because she doesn't dwell on that. She loves people, cares about them and gives her whole life to people who never realize the pain she has suffered over, and over.

Don's life to me is one of the finest examples I have ever seen of unconditional love, and ironically, of patience– because Don is not a patient man. He has learned patience through some tough experiences. Because he is a rational man, it's been difficult for him to deal with the anguish and the irrationality that depression can bring upon a person. These are courageous people. They will go forward, passing their courage on to their children. Their suffering has brought them a refinement of spirit and a wellspring of charity, which they will graciously share with others. (Funeral sermon used by permission of survivor)

In June of 1987, two men interviewed our family, one the producer of the PBS/BBC series "The Search for Mind." They were researching our family's bipolar history. In a follow-up letter they wrote:

"As a result of speaking with you, we have made sure that the danger of suicide among depressed people is made clear in the film. We interviewed a number of people who have attempted suicide and several doctors who discuss the pervasive nature of suicide among depressed people."

On April 2001, I emerged from my twenty-fifth painful bout with depression. As always, it was horrific, black, debilitating and irrational. As usual, I was convinced that "this time" the blackness would not leave—this time that depression would remain. But like a miracle in two months it finally lifted and once again my world is filled with beauty, light, and my beloved family and precious friends. When I am "well," I feel very willing to share our family's experiences. My hope is that my story—and Cory's—might help prevent other such tragedies and provide added insights and comfort to those who are struggling with the pain of suicide or severe depression.

In Emily Dickinson's words (1830-1886)

Not In Vain

If I can stop one heart from breaking,
I shall not live in vain:
If I can ease one life the aching,
Or cool one pain
Or help one fainting robin
Unto his nest again,
I shall not live in vain

(*101 Famous Poems*, p. 30, Pub. Reilley & Lee Co. 1958)

"What's the Point?"

Erica

By Bill

It's been about four months since my daughter, Erica, hung herself. Let me tell you a little about her. My wife, Deann, and I had been married ten years before we were able to have children. Through the wonders of medicine and a lot of prayers we were able to have twins, Erica and her sister. Erica brought a lot of joy to our lives, although she had many challenges. She was born with a hearing impairment, scoliosis, and asthma. In her youth, she had an operation to restore her hearing, which accidentally severed the nerves in one side of her face. She felt very self-conscious because the paralysis took away half of her smile. In her younger pictures she had a very beautiful, full smile, but after the surgery people made fun of her and teased her.

I miss Erica very much. We spent a lot of time together as a family. I didn't go out with the guys to do sports or hunting--I went out with my family. Erica played basketball and softball and I was her coach. She took piano lessons too. Music was hard for her because of her hearing impairment, but she did it and I went to her recitals. We took family vacations every year to give our daughters exposure to different places and people. Those were fun times. We tried to help our daughters know our Lord and Savior and understand that they are daughters of God. We went to church and prayed together. I had many talks with Erica during the weeks before her suicide. I knew something was wrong, but there was a lot I didn't understand.

Prior to her death, I learned that she had been raped many times on dates. I found out about other problems she had also. She dealt with her problems in her own way and began making unsuitable life choices. Her attitude about the Savior and the Church changed and eventually she stopped going. When I talked with her I could tell she was dealing with depression, hate, and discontent. As soon as we discovered these things she began therapy and was placed on medication.

My wife and I loved Erica deeply. We tried to understand what she was going through and did everything we could think of to help her. I believe that she knew we loved her, but this didn't stop her from taking her life.

Erica hung herself with our dog, Buddy's, leash. She threw one end of the leash over a plank in the basement ceiling and placed the other end around her neck. Then she knelt on her bed and leaned onto the leash until she went unconscious. She died. I don't think it was painful. When my wife discovered her she was kneeling on the bed with Buddy's leash around her neck and Buddy, her dog was on the bed beside her. My wife called me after finding Erica. I told her to call 911. I immediately came home. I pulled in the driveway behind the police and paramedics. I had to remove Buddy while the paramedics worked on Erica. It has bothered me to think she could have sat up anytime and saved her life. She must have been in great emotional pain. We still have Buddy now. He helps us deal with Erica's death. Sometimes, he stares off into the room. We think he might see Erica.

Erica died on the 21st of the month. Every month since then on the 21st I've relived driving into the driveway, going down the stairs, and seeing Erica hanging there.

The first few days after her death we had many people comforting and helping us. The bishop gave me a priesthood blessing and together we blessed my wife and daughters. We received extra strength to deal with the viewing and the funeral. It got harder as time went on. The phone didn't ring as much and people stopped visiting. Then reality set in and I started feeling the grief and sorrow keenly. When it hit me I'd cry and take deep breaths to bring down my blood pressure and help me relax. I couldn't get what happened out of my mind.   Church was especially difficult. I would sit with my eyes closed through the hymns and the talks. Sometimes I would just sob. If someone asked me if I were having a bad day, I'd say, "Every day is bad."

Going back to work was good for me. When I first went back all I could see was Erica's face. When the paramedics carried her out of the house in a body bag I asked them to unzip it so that I could kiss her lifeless face. I couldn't get that picture out of my mind. I eventually brought a lot of pictures of her growing up and on vacations to work. I put them on my desk, on my wall, and in my day planner. I wanted to be reminded of the happy memories, not the last few moments of her life. It helped. People I work with have been very understanding and helpful. Some of them have acted as sounding boards. Since Erica died, they have been less critical of me and it's made my work less stressful.

We haven't felt much guilt because we'd been very devoted to Erica and to helping her with her special needs. We have felt a tremendous amount of sorrow and grief, however. The last couple of months things have improved somewhat. At first I tried to figure out why it happened and I had many questions about Erica's death. A friend who lost his wife to suicide told me, "There is a plan that you're not aware of. Don't dwell on the whys. Look to the future and focus on the family left behind. Erica is in a better place. You'll kill yourself if you focus on the unanswered questions." I finally realized that some things are not meant for me to know. The unanswered questions don't bother me so much anymore.

Since Erica's death, I've been trying to help my family. My wife is on antidepressant medication now. Her sister took her life and another sister tried to kill herself earlier. Depression and suicide run in her family. I try to listen to her and to spend a lot of time with her. I try not to lecture her. It's hard sometimes, but I love her. Our younger daughter, Jessica, was quite close to Erica. We recently learned that one of Jessica's friends was contemplating suicide. It was wearing Jessica down to have her friends coming to her with thoughts of dying. I listen to her and talk to her about her feelings. We've become a lot closer as a father and daughter. I try to do what I can to help my wife and daughters as well as to deal with my own pain. Sometimes I'm overwhelmed and I think, "What's the point?" I give priesthood blessings to my family. Sometimes I'm spiritually ready and sometimes I'm not, but I just do what I can and accept myself for that.

Some things just aren't as important to me any more. Before Erica's death, I would think, "I need to do this or that "--like be to work on time and make more money for the family. Now I spend more time with my wife and girls. I'll wait up for my girls to come home and talk to them about how things went. The next morning I'll go into work late and make it up at another time. The job and other things are secondary now. I've learned that life is too short to worry about things that don't really matter.

My wife and I have joined a support group of other families who have experienced suicide. It's very comforting to talk to them and we've become good friends. If I get emotional, then I get emotional. I can deal with tears and most of my friends can too. Tears are good. In the past two weeks there have been four more suicides in our community. We've been trying to help their families and it helps us too.

Erica's suicide has been a wake-up call for me. Life is tentative. You can have someone one day and the next day you don't. It makes me realize that I have to do everything I can to fulfill my stewardship as a father and husband. I believe that the Church is true and that God speaks to our prophet. I believe that Joseph Smith was a prophet. I know this. I also know that there is a Satan and that he has a lot of tools. I've felt his presence. I rely on prayers and I know the Lord answers prayers. I don't believe I'll get all the answers about Erica's death in this life. I don't understand why some things happen or why I have to deal with them, but I have been comforted and strengthened to cope with my challenges. As painful as it has been, I think I'm learning "the point."

UNDERSTANDING THE HEALING PROCESS: DEPRESSION AND LONELINESS

Most suicidal people and survivors of suicide experience sadness and depression. Depression is said to be the "common cold" of modern life. It ranks second, after heart disease as the most disabling ailment in the Western countries.

Depression can range from a temporary feeling of sadness to a very serious chemical imbalance in the brain. The more serious types of depression are considered a mental illness. Depression can occur because of a variety of factors, including substance abuse, mental illness, conflicting lifestyles, or the death of a loved one. The bad news is that depression is common; the good news is that people often respond well to treatment, both biological and psychological. Depression left untreated can be devastating and even fatal.

When suicide survivors realize that bargaining has not worked and the struggle to ward off reality has not been effective, an overwhelming depression can take over. This is commonly when the full force of the loss is experienced and is accompanied by crying and intense emotional pain. The more serious types of depression are characterized by the following feelings:

♦ You may feel lost, empty, alone, reclusive and restless.

♦ You may feel mentally and physically drained with nothing to give.

♦ You may feel helpless and powerless. You may feel emotionally paralyzed and inept.

♦ Your sleeping and eating patterns may change drastically.

♦ You may have thoughts of: "Why bother? Things will never get better or be the same." This may prevent you from performing even routine tasks. You may not want to go out in public.

♦ You may feel like a failure, and experience self-pity, despair, and a loss of hope.

♦ You may have a desire to die. You may also feel that you can't make it on your own.

♦ You may begin self destructive or self-defeating behaviors.

♦ You may feel consumed with grief and so overwhelmed that you struggle to make decisions.

Crying is a good way to express sorrow. It relieves some of the emotional pain, washes away sadness, and heals. Tears and funerals allow you to be sad and reach some closure. Crying is a sign of strength when used as part of the grieving process, but if prolonged, crying can become a chronic behavior that does not effectively promote grieving. Accept that it is okay to feel sad and tearful at times and to talk about those feelings. It is part of the healing process.

Elder Jeffrey R. Holland emphasized the healing power of tears in speaking to the widow and family at the funeral of a close friend, Karl, who took his life:

> I ask us not to hide our grief, especially you, Susie, and the children and the grandchildren when they come to hear this story. There is no pretense here that this is all wonderful, that there is no sorrow or disappointment. Tears are appropriate. What anger you feel, get that out, let it go and send it on its way. These emotions are real and we won't do each other any service if we pretend there is no pain in this. Tears are appropriate. "Thou shalt live together in love, insomuch that thou shalt weep for the loss of them that die." *(Doctrine & Covenants 42:45)*

The only thing worse than losing Karl now and in this way – unexpectedly and without our preparation – would be not to care, to act like it didn't even matter. Tears are the price we pay for love in this world. You shed them as you need to and you'll be healing sooner and feeling God's strength more with His love upon you. Karl made a mistake but it is not our role to pass judgment.

"I, the Lord, will forgive whom I will forgive, but of you (and of me), it is required to forgive all men." (Elder Jeffrey R. Holland, funeral service remarks, used by permission)

When a loved one dies, part of us dies too. Because that person cannot be replaced, loneliness in separation is the price we pay for loving. Loneliness may last a lifetime when an anniversary, a place, a song, or a flower brings back the aching painful memories. You will feel the disappointment of not having that special person there to share in the family's activities, events, joys and sorrows. However, by accepting the loneliness and realizing the depths of your love, you can learn to become more sensitive to others in their losses. By reaching out to others and placing your hurt, your sensitivity, and your compassion at the service of others, you will discover a way to help yourself as related in the story of "Lisa", whose mother made it her mission to minister to those in depression.

It takes courage to place your sensitivity and compassion at the service of others, but it is part of the key to helping yourself. Use your pain to reach out to others. It will become a creative and transforming love. As the Savior said: "If any man will come after me, let him deny himself, and take up his cross daily, and follow me. For whosoever will save his life shall lose it: but whosoever will lose his life for my sake, the same shall save it." (Luke 9:23-24) King Benjamin in Mosiah 2:17 made the definitive statement about service: "And behold, I tell you these things that ye may learn wisdom; that ye may learn that when ye are in the service of your fellow beings ye are only in the service of your God."

Depression and loneliness may reoccur in the months and years after a suicide. Survivors have found serving others helps them heal. You can come to know the Savior and feel of His love for you by seeking out someone you can minister to who is hurting. Pray to find someone to help. Listen to them and be their friend. You can enlist your family's help in service projects, which will help each member heal. Service to others will help you forget your own sadness and loneliness. Elder Neal A. Maxwell spoke of the importance of service:

> We, more than others, should carry jumper and tow cables not only in our cars, but also in our hearts, by which means we can send the needed boost or charge of encouragement or added momentum to mortal neighbors. *(The Neal A. Maxwell Quote Book, "Service," p. 312)*

> To withdraw into our private sanctuaries not only deprives others of our love, our talents, and our service, but it also deprives us of chances to serve, to love and to be loved. *(The Neal A. Maxwell Quote Book, "Service," p. 314)*

HELPS FOR HEALING

The path of healing in this stage will be in taking small steps each day to return to normal activities of daily living and in finding something positive that is happening in your family. Many survivors have found the following tasks to be helpful:

◆ Do your best to take care of yourself.

◆ Try to get sufficient sleep and eat regular well-balanced meals.

◆ Exercise regularly.

◆ Find the listening ear of a good friend. Get a priesthood blessing. Caring friends and extended family can provide emotional support and help in the healing process.

♦ Find others you can serve.

♦ Develop resources and a support system that encourage the positive changes in you and in your life. These may be ecclesiastical leaders, close friends, survivors of suicide support groups, and mental health groups.

However, if the symptoms of depression continue for several weeks and interfere with daily living activities, you may need professional help, which could include temporary medication and/or counseling from a mental health professional.

Chapter 9

ACCEPTANCE AND HOPE

"What I gained from losing Brian."

BRIAN

By Margie Holmes

Brian was our firstborn child. I vividly remember driving home very slowly and carefully from the hospital, my husband at the wheel, Brian cradled in my arms. We were filled with the desire to protect this child from harm and raise him well. I was surprised at how overwhelming the responsibility of a completely dependent child was to me. Still, I was confident that my strong desire to be a good parent and our love would be enough to sustain his healthy development.

Brian was a strong-willed, brilliant, creative, affectionate boy whose interests and temperament were different enough from those around him to make it difficult for him to be accepted. Age sixteen was a turning point in his young life. He seemed to reject most of the values we held dear. He stopped attending church, his grades dropped, and his appearance changed as he found new friends. He was angry much of the time, and there was a great deal of conflict in our home. We knew he had some involvement with alcohol, tobacco, drugs, and the occult. To this day we're not sure how deep that involvement was or to what degree he suffered from depression or other emotional illnesses that went undiagnosed and untreated.

A month after Brian's eighteenth birthday, The police called me at work to say that he was dead. After drinking late into the night with friends, he had taken some sleeping pills and had finally gone to bed at about 5:00 a.m. Early the next afternoon, the people he was staying with had tried to wake him and had found him dead. I don't know if Brian intended to die and knew exactly what amounts in combination would kill him or if he wasn't thinking very clearly and made a fatal mistake. There is evidence to support either conclusion. All of the uncertainty surrounding his behavior and his death made coming to terms with the situation very difficult.

I had always hoped that time and experience would soften Brian's heart and help him return to productive and happy living. I had always kept a prayer in my heart that his father and I--or the bishop, or someone, anyone--would be inspired to know how to help him. There was much about Brian to love--our last words to each other were 'I love you'--and I felt that his goodness would eventually quiet the rebellion in his soul. Never had I thought that he would not have the chance to turn his life around. Now it was all over here, and the phrase "everlastingly too late" (Helaman 13:38) pulsed through my brain again and again.

My reaction to his death involved a complex interplay of feelings. At first there was a kind of numbness, shock, bewilderment, and disbelief. There was a sense of unreality, of watching myself go through the motions of making funeral arrangements, dealing with the police, and letting friends and family know what had happened. This numbness was interspersed with intense feelings of anguish. My chest and stomach would fill with a dark purple, tight pain and I would sob and groan, especially in the shower where the warm water on my body helped release emotion. I also felt a great deal of shame, an overwhelming sense of failure at not providing Brian with what he needed to survive. A few days after his death, as I was sorting dirty laundry I saw his face for a few moments at the end of the hall. He was smiling softly and looked very clean. Many times during the following years I returned to that vision for reassurance. On the day of his funeral the music, prayers, and gentle words of friends filled me with peace, calmness, and comfort and I felt sustained by the Spirit of the Lord.

As time went on and the reality of death became clearer, feelings of longing became very strong. I would have given anything to see Brian again, to touch him, to talk to him. I was filled with regrets about our conflicts and our inability to get the help he needed. I could remember clearly every mistake I had made with him but I couldn't give myself credit for the years of devotion I had lavished on him--the stories read, the costumes made, the chauffeuring, the hugs, the praise, the birthday parties. I carried a lot of guilt and although I wasn't angry at the woman who gave him the pills or the acquaintances who encouraged his destructive choices, I couldn't forgive myself or my husband for what we saw as our failures. We had a tremendous drive to make sense of all of this, to understand it, to find out what had happened and why. Placing blame and feeling guilt were a part of trying to make sense of a senseless act.

As the months and years passed, I had a lot of concern about Brian's well-being. It's hard being a mother when there's nothing you can do for your child and you can't even get a letter to let you know how he's doing. I wondered if he was suffering, if he had been healed, if he was experiencing joy, if he was in the company of those who loved him. I worried about his spiritual well being. I alternated between thinking that he was suffering for his sins, that he was in Satan's clutches and would never be free on the one hand, and on the other hand that he wouldn't be punished for his choices because he had suffered enough in this life to pay for them, and that perhaps I and others were largely responsible for his problems anyway. My grieving was prolonged by my desires to take upon myself any suffering owed by my son, so that he wouldn't have to endure it.

In my guilt and grief, I sought comfort from God. My need to understand life and death, justice and mercy, was desperate. My prayers were anguished, and my worship at church and at the temple was exceedingly sorrowful. I felt that I had failed in a monumental way in the most important task of my life and that God had abandoned me at the time of my greatest need. I'd followed the rules to the best of my ability, but it just hadn't worked out the way I'd been led to expect. Deep down I'd really thought that Mormons were special. If we tried hard enough to do what was right, terrible things wouldn't happen to us.

I directed much of my energy to reaching God, seeking comfort and understanding. I wanted to know what Brian's death meant to my relationship with God, my son, and my fellow human beings. Scripture study was one of the means through which I sought solace and insight. Rather than finding solace, however, I found judgment and condemnation. I needed a forgiving Father who loved me regardless of my failure and who responded to my pleas for healing and mercy. Although I tried to focus on the numerous passages that portray God in this way, my guilt would not allow me to transcend the condemnatory messages with which they were interspersed. I read, for example, that he who "remaineth and dieth in his sins . . . receiveth . . . an everlasting punishment" (Mosiah *2:33)* which "doth fill his breast with guilt, and pain, and anguish, which is like an unquenchable fire" (Mosiah 2:38). My mind filled with pictures of Brian suffering eternally, and my own contribution to that suffering seemed unforgivable. In spite of the pain it caused me, I continued reading the scriptures hoping to receive revelation. Eventually I learned to find comfort and spiritual guidance in the scriptures, but it took several years (for an account of this process, see Margie Holmes "With Great Mercies Will I Gather Thee," *Ensign,* January 1992)

Attending Church and working in the temple gradually became less difficult as well and soothing spiritual experiences occurred there. I was in Relief Society and Primary presidencies continuously for more than six years after Brian's death. Serving in this way helped me regain feelings of worthiness. I couldn't be a complete failure if the Lord saw fit to use me in his Church. Being Relief Society president also allowed me to find some meaning in my suffering. The increased capacity to love and understand others I had gained because of it was called upon frequently.

Kind friends and neighbors listened to me sort through my confused feelings, wept with me, gave me blessings, and showered me with food, cards, gifts, and love. One friend in particular helped me discover the nature of my deepest fears: that Brian was in Satan's power because of his involvement in the occult. I also met periodically with a therapist whose insight and sensitivity eased my way through the process of facing those fears, searching once more through all of the sources available to me for information about what had happened and why, and finally letting the unanswerable questions go. After six years of resisting, I also began taking antidepressant medication. For me it was the final step towards recovery and experiencing joy in living once again.

In the months after Brian's death, I also experienced a loss of ambition. The professional identity that I had clung to so fiercely to prevent being devoured by my roles as wife and mother became much less important. My work was helpful as a means of respite from grieving, but for several years my efforts were channeled primarily into restoring my sense of myself as a decent human being. Mostly that meant allowing myself time with good friends who loved me and time to read and think. The value of meaningful work gradually returned and my accomplishments became an additional source of healing.

An emotion that surprised me was a deadening of feeling toward my other five children. So much of my energy was tied up in mourning Brian's loss, even wanting to join him, that enjoying my other children was difficult. Ironically, the events that taught me with great clarity the worth of a soul, even a troubled, difficult soul, were blunting my feelings toward other precious souls. For a long time, I felt like I had a foot in both worlds, this one and the next. Eventually this phase ended, however, and I was left with the exquisite awareness of the goodness of my children, an appreciation for the very ordinary things that they did, and the ability to love them for who they are, rather than what I had hoped they would be. That is Brian's legacy to his younger siblings-- wiser, more patient, appreciative parents, and enhanced gratitude for ordinary things. Small things that had annoyed us before seemed very insignificant now. A missed piano lesson, an imperfect household chore, a B instead of an A grade--what did they matter? Our children were alive and learning and growing. They were good citizens and would grow up to marry, have children, and hold down a job. Mundane things that we had assumed happened to everyone now seemed like great blessings.

One of the most difficult aspects of Brian's death for me was the wedge it drove between my husband and me. Our wounds were so deep and our vulnerability so great that we were unable to be sources of strength for one another. Our paths of grieving and healing were separate. The support I felt from friends was not as readily available to him and he was not as willing to seek therapy or explore some of the spiritual ideas from which I found solace. For him, writing in his journal and listening to classical music were beneficial. Part of our difficulty was the blame I placed on him for Brian's difficulties. I had to learn to forgive him and myself for immaturity, lack of wisdom and all of the other weaknesses that are overcome only through experience.

In the end, I learned that none of us can do everything right. All of us sin and fall short of the glory of God. When Ethiopian children were starving to death and Jews by the millions had died in the gas chambers, why did I think I should be spared suffering? God loves the Muslim woman pregnant through rape just as much as he loves me. I developed a kinship with suffering people everywhere. The prisoner serving time for dealing drugs has a mother who weeps for him too. The homeless, the mentally ill, the criminal are not from a different race. They're someone's sons and daughters. They are my brothers and my sisters and we are all wounded by life. We are all in need of God's grace, His love and his mercy.

Eventually I came to understand that Christ's atonement applies to me, to my son, to my husband--not just to others. I did everything I knew how, and it wasn't enough. That's why we have our Savior. What a relief that has been to me. I don't have to do it by myself. I can love others because I am so grateful for the love that has been extended to me and I want to return it. I can hold the hands of my fellow-sufferers. Most of the time I can't fix anything.

But I can love, I can accept, I can understand, I can withhold judgment, I can cry with my friends. I can offer my heart, which truly is broken and softened, and my spirit, which truly is contrite. I don't worry about my image any more. When I failed at the most important task of my life and found myself acceptable before God and loved by my friends, it freed me up to be more authentically who I am.

I don't worry much about Brian now. I trust that my Father and Mother in Heaven love Brian much more than I am capable of loving him. Surely they will provide him with the experiences he needs to become the righteous, magnificent Son of God that is his potential. If he is in prison, surely those who love him have taught him and he will be able to choose the light, if he has not already done so. For me, this life is not so much a test as a school where we learn the good from the evil by our own experience. The suffering we endure here serves to turn our hearts to God and to one another, to prepare us for further growth in the life to come where Jesus Christ waits with open arms to embrace us, heal us, and lead us to the next stage of our growth.

"OH DANNY BOY"

DANNY

By Jane Ann Bradford Olsen,

When Danny was a baby, I would listen with joy to the soothing voice of my husband singing the Irish ballad, *Oh Danny Boy*, as he rocked our Danny to sleep. Twenty-three years later, the song held a haunting sadness for me as I listened to it at Danny's funeral. How could Danny be gone? What had happened to this once sensitive and happy child who had found such joy in bringing me flowers and was so reluctant to stray very far from the warmth and safety of his family and home? Why was there no comfort in the flowers that surrounded his casket?

It was during a dark Saturday morning hour that Danny shot himself through the heart. Later that morning, my husband, Paul, found him lying on his bed and called me to his bedroom. The shock, pain and grief I felt as I embraced my son's body cannot be written.

How do a mother and a father survive such a loss? How do you face the feelings of guilt and failure? How do you deal with the reality that it is now everlastingly too late to help this child work through his earthly struggles? What did the Destroyer have to do with the act? Did Danny's use of alcohol bring about his death? What role did depression play? How do you find answers to all the desperate questions that pound through your heart and head?

During Danny's first year in college, he began drinking alcohol. His lifelong plans to serve a mission for the Church were set aside. He left college and joined the Navy, but a medical disability sent him home. That fateful Saturday morning Danny ultimately gave up on the challenges of this life. The note beside his bed spoke of wanting to be a better person, of being emotionally torn apart, of coming to the end of what he could bear in this life, of going to a higher judge; the highest judge Himself, Jesus Christ.

It has been more than a year since Danny's death and I can now look back on the process of grieving and healing and attempt to share some of the things I have experienced. It is the hope and prayer of my heart that I can describe the workings of the Spirit in my life. I know that the Holy Ghost walked me through this time.

When I was a young mother with six young children, I recognized the blessings that surrounded me. Everything in my life seemed almost too perfect. I learned from the whisperings of the Spirit that this was a time to build a strong relationship with my Heavenly Father, my Savior Jesus Christ, my husband, and my children. I devoted the majority of my time and talents to being a wife, a mother, and a homemaker. I was continually educating myself to succeed in this role. Above all, I wanted to center everything we did on Jesus Christ and make Him the foundation of our lives. This time in my life was a season of growing. I could never have comprehended then what my season of testing would be like. I will be forever grateful for the reservoir of strength that was filled during those growing years.

During that time I learned how the Spirit was teaching me. Often I recognized the influence of the Spirit only after it had moved me in a certain direction. I would look back with an "ah-hah" understanding as I realized how I had been led. Soon I came to pray for this divine influence. My spiritual eyes were opened and I began to recognize the guiding influence of the Lord in my life. I took time to stop, to listen, to be in tune, and to realize that my prayers were being answered.

After the initial shock of Danny's death, I turned to prayer. I never doubted that my Father in Heaven and my Savior loved me. I never cried out in sorrow or anger against them. More than any other time in my life I wanted to be spiritually in tune to their influence.

The day Danny died, my husband, Paul, phoned our other five children. They were spread out from California to Missouri. Before Saturday night all had arrived at our home in Utah. I recognized the strength they brought with them and welcomed it as the beginning of divine help. As we knelt in our bedroom, the circle included our five children and the eternal companions of the three that were married. Through the years we had "circled up" many times to search for divine guidance. Two years before Danny's death, I had drawn on this combined strength to help me undergo a liver transplant.

Each person in the circle felt safe to openly and honestly share their feelings. There were many expressions of anguish, anger, and tears along with the unanswerable questions of why Danny had chosen to do this. These feelings of sadness and confusion began to yield to the comforting influence of the Holy Ghost, who brought peace and the beginning of understanding. That night ended with expressions of love, prayers and priesthood blessings.

Through the years we have been able to establish an atmosphere of trust and open communication in our family. It is my testimony that this, along with our commitment to the Savior and the Gospel, played a key role in the healing process. The warmth of the Spirit of our Heavenly Father and His Beloved Son wrapped around us. Their divine presence was stronger than I had ever experienced before. I not only felt an outpouring of peace, but also of knowledge.

The things the Spirit taught us are precious and sacred. During the time before the funeral, the veil was very thin. We came to know that Danny's spirit was near. We shared our impressions and experiences and were drawn together in a spirit of oneness. From this point on I never felt that I was facing my pain alone. The combined strength and testimony of our family helped me stay tuned to the divine guidance of the Spirit. The anger that some of the family had felt toward Satan was replaced by a desire to know the Lord's will for us. Shortly after my oldest son, Randy, was told that Danny had died, he heard the Spirit of the Lord whisper these words to his mind: "Vengeance is mine alone." As one who recognized the work of opposition in Danny's life, Randy wrote the following words:

> The equation of what happened to Danny is very complicated. Some of these factors were: a deep, recurring frustration that he could not permanently break his habits and change his life, the influence of alcohol and the cloud that it casts on a person's reasoning, and being ashamed of his failures especially after making a new start.

> Danny felt all these influences and others in the hours before he decided he was going to leave mortality. One of the other influences that he felt that night was that of spirits who follow Satan. They desperately wanted him to do what he did. Danny will have to overcome the habits that left him vulnerable to those influences, but he is not responsible for the portion of his act that resulted from those evil influences.

Danny's experiences with evil spirits were frightening to him and to me. One night he quietly shook me awake. I got out of bed and went with him so we could talk. His face was drained of color. He had parked his truck on a hill overlooking our property. There in the darkness he had seen several evil spirits. He rolled up the windows, turned on the key, but by the time he started the engine, they were on the hood of his truck. He was able to drive home, but the experience left him pale and shaken and he wanted a priesthood blessing. I returned to the bedroom and awakened his father. After the blessing, my husband went with Danny to his bedroom and slept on the floor next to his bed. On another occasion, Danny asked his brother, Stephen, to use his priesthood to command the evil spirits he felt in his bedroom to leave.

As we prepared for Danny's funeral every member of our family expressed a desire to be as involved as possible in the funeral arrangements and to delegate only a few things to others.

Three brothers and two sisters prepared to speak at Danny's funeral. Two sisters-in-law and a brother-in-law would offer the prayers. Danny's father would dedicate the grave. The pallbearers would be Danny's brothers, his two sisters, and two close childhood friends. All of us gathered at the mortuary. Danny's body was dressed by his brothers and again we had family prayer. There was a healing catharsis in all these actions.

Along the way there were many "little hugs" from Heavenly Father that I recognized and was thankful for. I will mention just a few: Our Bishop knelt with us in Danny's room for prayer before the sheriff and mortician came. He was very sensitive in waiting until I was ready for these men to be called in. Ward members, family, and friends came without hesitation. A sweet daughter-in-law spent hours producing a combination of music and slides of Danny's life. A dear young friend from Mexico put herself in charge of the well being of the grandchildren. Another friend came to the mortuary to comb my hair. Throughout the entire viewing at the mortuary, a brother stayed in the background lending me silent strength. A friend came to the funeral with his video camera to film Danny's services for later viewing.

I will be eternally grateful for these arms that reached out to hold me. It reminded me of the quote from President Spencer W. Kimball that I love so much:

> *"God does notice us, and He watches over us. But it is usually through another person that He meets our needs. Therefore, it is vital that we serve each other."*
> ("The Abundant Life," *Ensign, Oct. 1985, p.3)*

Early in this experience the Spirit focused my attention back to the April 1992 General Conference. As Elder Boyd K. Packer was speaking, the Spirit was teaching me. After the conference I discussed Elder Packer's words in depth with my husband and my children. I carefully read his words in the Ensign and listened to them over and over when I received the Conference tapes. I knew his message applied to us and to Danny's struggle. He had said:

> It is a great challenge to raise a family in the darkening mists of our moral environment. We emphasize that the greatest work you will ever do will be within the walls of your own home. The measure of our success as parents, however, will not rest solely on how our children turn out. That judgment would be just only if we could raise our families in a perfectly moral environment, and that now is not possible. It is not uncommon for responsible parents to lose one of their children, for a time, to influences over which they have no control. They agonize over rebellious sons or daughters. They are puzzled over why they are so helpless when they have tried so hard to do what they should. It is my conviction that those wicked influences one day will be overruled.

> The Prophet Joseph Smith declared--and he never taught a more comforting doctrine-that the eternal sealings of faithful parents and the divine promises made to them for valiant service in the Cause of Truth, would save not only themselves, but likewise their posterity. Though some of the sheep may wander, the eye of the Shepherd is upon them, and sooner or later they will feel the tentacles of Divine Providence reaching out after them and drawing them back to the fold. Either in this life or the life to come, they will return. They will have to pay their debt to justice; they will suffer for their sins; and may tread a thorny path; but if it leads them at last, like the penitent Prodigal, to a loving and forgiving Father's heart and home, the painful experience will not have been in vain. Pray for your careless and disobedient children; hold on to them with your faith. Hope on, trust on.

And from Brigham Young:

> Let the father and mother, who are members of this
> Church and Kingdom, take a righteous course, and strive
> with all their might never to do a wrong, but to do good all
> their lives; if they have one child or one hundred children,
> if they conduct themselves towards them as they should,
> binding them to the Lord by their faith and prayers, I care
> not where those children go, they are bound up to their
> parents by an everlasting tie, and no power of earth or hell
> can separate them from their parents in eternity; they will
> return again to the fountain from whence they sprang.
> *(Discourses of Brigham Young,* p. 208*)*

(Elder Boyd K. Packer, *Ensign,* May, 1992, Conference
Report © 2000 Intellectual Reserve Inc.*)*

> Our son, Ronny, quoted all of these words in his
> funeral address. Then Ronny said:

> And with that doctrine and that feeling, I wish to
> declare to all within the sound of my voice and let it be
> known throughout all the expanses of eternity that Daniel
> Bradford Olsen belongs to Paul R. and Jane Ann Olsen and
> it is our intent that we will fulfill the promises and the
> requirements of this law and we will have our brother!

> And so how is it possible? Because of the suffering
> of Jesus Christ. Because He entered the Garden of
> Gethsemane. Because He went lower than we can
> comprehend. Because in His agony in His lying on the
> ground in the blood which came from every pore, there was
> a place of suffering for us in our family. I don't understand,
> but I have faith, and the Spirit comforts me. I thank my
> Savior this day for His love and His mercy.

Danny's funeral was a witness to me, to my husband, and to
our family (including Danny) that all was not lost. Our son,

Randy, bore testimony that all of our efforts on Danny's part were not wasted. He said:

> Danny needs and he will use all of the training that he received in our home in what he is doing now. Everything that Mama and Daddy did counts. It counts now and he will use it in this life he is living now. Mama and Daddy, you equipped Danny well for this last camp-out!

Every person spoke with conviction and witness that our family would be eternal. This was the greatest healing message that I received, and I knew it was from the Lord.

After the funeral our family continued to huddle together. We wanted to keep ourselves in tune with the outpouring of the Spirit and the light of personal revelation. No one allowed any distractions; no television, no news, no shopping. Just as I was inquiring heavenward: "Is this all, dear Father?" He sent us a very real witness of Danny's well being. This personal revelation came to our family through my visiting teacher, who had been one of Danny's adult friends. She saw a vision of Danny with his paternal grandfather, which remains very sacred to each family member. I believe it is within the realm of each family who goes through this experience to receive their own personal witness of the well being of their loved one.

The time arrived when we had to part. We faced it reluctantly. We were filled with a desire to keep the strength we had received. We met together one last time to voice our commitment to fortify each other as we went forward without Danny. We understood Satan's subtle weapons, especially his wedge of discouragement and despair. Because we knew that Satan is a powerful opponent, we talked about putting on the whole armor of God.

As our family said farewell and my husband went back to work, I knew my time of testing had arrived. I wondered if I would be O.K. During that first year I talked a great deal about my feelings. My therapists were the Spirit of the Holy Ghost, my dear husband, and my family. I continued to feel cradled, but still it was a yo-yo year of hurting and healing.

There were heart-wrenching moments of unbelief and sadness as I relived Danny's death. When I got shingles, I took a serious look at the stress I was feeling and the Spirit urged me to hold on to my health. I returned to my morning walks and making fresh juice. I realized that I needed both exercise and energy to heal. I approached the problem of restless nights by turning to the taped voice of an inspired teacher. His message about the Prophet Joseph Smith and his voice helped me to listen, to relax, to forget, and to sleep. I didn't resist grieving, but when my son, Stephen, said: "Mama, don't grieve too much or Danny's progress will be slowed", I promised myself not to keep reviewing the "If onlys", such as, "If only we had gotten professional counseling for Danny..."

One day my daughter, Kristine, came to have prayer with me because she had a spiritual prompting that Danny was missing his family. Praying and pondering that day about Danny missing us brought forgiveness. I whispered over and over to him: "It's all right. It's all right. Everything will be all right."

My children called and wrote letters. I looked forward to my son-in-law's "How are you doing" interviews and my mother's cheerful visits. I remembered a theme from a Life Management seminar my family had participated in over a year ago: "The only way out is through." I knew I was making progress.

In the beginning, I wondered how I could ever return to "dressing up" and "going out", but going shopping, going to the hair dresser, planning meals and keeping house all got me going again. Slowly I began to go through the routine of such simple chores as doing laundry and shopping without shedding tears. My grocery list had always had a section of Danny's special requests.

The decision to return right away to Church and to my calling to teach the Gospel Doctrine class was important. I was met with loving eyes, warm hands, and healing hugs. After nine months had gone by, I accepted an additional calling to serve on a curriculum writing committee for the Church. All these things helped with the healing process.

My husband built a wonderful memorial in a grove of oaks on our property. It was a place where Danny went when he wanted to be outside with nature, a place where Danny had built warm fires and coaxed us outside to laugh and be ourselves. Now it is a place of memory with a plaque that reads: DANNY'S PLACE. It has become a place for happy family gatherings around a permanent fire pit surrounded by beautiful trees and benches.

I was prompted by the Spirit to compile a book on Danny's life for each of us. Working on this Danny Book was a healing experience. Page after page captured Danny the baby and his innocence, Danny the boy and his flowers, Danny the youth and his searching, and finally Danny the man and the masks. The book was a sad project, but it helped me look at the whole of Danny's life. Slowly the tragic end ceased to swallow up everything else. Now the book is a treasure for us all.

My youngest daughter, Laura Ann, made plans to go on a mission. While she was in the Missionary Training Center, she became aware of Danny's presence as she fasted and prayed for a stronger testimony of the Prophet Joseph Smith. Danny always loved to read and listen to stories about Joseph Smith. Now he was allowed to share his testimony with Laura Ann that Joseph Smith is indeed a prophet of God.

The experience of death was new to our grandchildren. The loss of Uncle Danny caused them to worry that other family members might also die. These young concerns prompted us to plan a summer family reunion. As we pondered how to help each child feel protected and safe, we were inspired to involve both children and adults in an Armor of God Ceremony. The grandchildren were fascinated with the idea of building a castle, wearing armor, coming to the ceremony on a horse, and being knighted. Grandpa supervised the building of a castle from a large pile of rocks that had been left on our property. Each grandchild helped and, wonder of wonders, the dream became a reality.

The moment of gathering was solemn and exciting. The children learned about the war in heaven and the protection we need on this earth from Satan. They memorized the spiritual meaning of the armor of God from Doctrine and Covenants 27 and Ephesians 6. They were clothed with armor and knighted a Saturday's Warrior by Grandpa Olsen with a sword that had belonged to Danny. We all felt the safety and protection of our Father in Heaven as we held hands in a family circle and thanked Him for His armor.

We began to look forward to the opportunity to do Danny's endowment in the temple. Again a blessing came from heaven. My husband, Paul, was called to be a veil worker at the Provo Temple. We decided that Danny's closest brother, Stephen, would do the endowment. Stephen prepared all of the records and documents for Danny's endowment. All of us were present on that sacred occasion when my husband was at the veil of the temple when Stephen went through for Danny. I cried tears of joy.

I humbly testify that challenges and afflictions in my life have brought me closer to Jesus Christ. For this reason, I consider them to be a blessing. I also know that the Savior strengthened me for those challenges that were meant to be an instrument for my growth. I have been guided through my trials and have received a greater vision and deeper appreciation for the suffering and sacrifice of my Savior, Jesus Christ, and a greater desire to be more sensitive and aware of the suffering of others.

One day, a framed quote arrived from my cousin, who was inspired to send it. It is a favorite of Elder Marion D. Hanks. It reads:

"To believe in God is to know that all the rules are fair and that there will be wonderful surprises."

I am filled with gratitude for the scriptures, for prayer, for the temple ceremony and for the promises to Danny, my husband and me, because of our temple sealing. Two scriptures speak to my heart and soul with new meaning. One is Doctrine and Covenants, Section 138:57-59:

> I beheld that the faithful elders of this dispensation, when they depart from mortal life, continue their labors in the preaching of the gospel of repentance and redemption, through the sacrifice of the Only Begotten Son of God, among those who are in darkness and under the bondage of sin in the great World of the spirits of the dead. The dead who repent will be redeemed, through obedience to the ordinances of the house of God. And after they have paid the penalty of their transgressions, and are washed clean, shall receive a reward according to their works, for they are heirs of salvation.

One of the Lord's great apostles who teaches these doctrines with hope and with promise is President Boyd K. Packer. In his October 1995 General Conference address, President Packer spoke to those who have made tragic mistakes and to parents who suffer unbearably because of the mistakes of wayward children. His address was entitled "The Brilliant Morning of Forgiveness". Surviving family members confront the question: "Can my loved one ever be forgiven?" To this question President Packer answered: "Yes!" He explained that relief from anguish and guilt could be earned through sincere repentance. That except for those who are guilty of perdition no offence is exempted from the promise of complete forgiveness. He reminded us that to earn forgiveness, restitution must be made. But there are some things that simply cannot be undone or restored, which is the very purpose of Christ's Atonement. He promised that when the desire to pay the "uttermost farthing" is firm, then the law of restitution is suspended and that obligation is transferred to the Lord. The Savior will settle those accounts.

Then President Packer repeated the promise wrought by the Atonement of Jesus Christ that complete forgiveness covers all addictions, all rebellions, all transgression, all apostasy, all crime, except for perdition.

No one knows how this will be accomplished, but we learn from Section 138 of the Doctrine & Covenants that the Lord's servants continue His work of redemption beyond the veil. (see Doctrine & Covenants 138)

President Packer quoted President Joseph F. Smith who commented on the mission of the Savior:

> "Jesus had not finished his work when his body was slain, neither did he finish it after his resurrection from the dead; although he had accomplished the purpose for which he then came to the earth, he had not fulfilled all his work. And when will he? Not until he has redeemed and saved every son and daughter of our father Adam that have been or ever will be born upon this earth to the end of time, except the sons of perdition. That is his mission." (Joseph F. Smith, *Gospel Doctrine* 5th ed., 1939. p. 442)

President Packer also quoted the Prophet Joseph Smith: *"There is never a time when the spirit is too old to approach God. All are within the reach of pardoning mercy, who have not committed the unpardonable sin."* (Teachings of the Prophet Joseph Smith, page 191.) (President Boyd K. Packer, *Ensign,* November 1995, pages 18-21© 1995 by Intellectual Reserve Incorporated.)

Another scripture which comforts us is 1 Nephi 21:15-16 (also Isaiah 49:15-16). The words from this passage are now engraved on Danny's headstone.

"I will not forget thee. Behold, I have graven thee upon the palms of my hands."

One day after I completed the Danny books, I walked beneath the majestic snow capped peaks of Mount Loafer and sang the words to the song, *Oh Danny Boy:*

> Oh Danny Boy, the pipes, the pipes are calling
> From glen to glen, and down the mountain side,
> The summer's gone, and all the roses falling,
> It's you, it's you must go, and I must bide.
> But come ye back when summer's in the meadow,
> Or when the valley's hushed and white with snow,
> It's I'll be here in sunshine or in shadow,
> Oh Danny Boy, oh Danny Boy, I love you so!

I thought of Ronny's words at Danny's funeral: "Danny found heavenly bastions of security with his family, good friends, and at times in his temple...the mountains." I knew that heavenly bastions of security surrounded Danny with his family and friends in the Spirit World. I knew that temples and mountains continued to bless his life." When I returned home I penned the following words to him:

> Dear Danny,
> Eternal horizons beckon to me,
> Since you stepped forth into eternity.
>
> I now stand on earth's narrow shore,
> Straining to see beyond the veil's thin door.
>
> But I have mountains yet to climb,
> Before the whisper: "It's your time."
>
> And I have commitments yet to keep,
> Before I close my eyes in sleep.
>
> And so I pray for you and me,
> And for everyone in our eternal family.

May each of us anxiously prepare!
Our family circle must have <u>no empty chair!</u>

I love you, Mama

Danny is still very much a part of our family. We continue to pray for him now just as fervently as we did when he was here. I know he is aware of our prayers. I know that the prayers of every member of our family are a great strength to him now.

There is hope! Hold on! Trust on! Remember your sons and your daughters are also the sons and daughters of Heavenly Father. He loves them too. He will join with you in a partnership to hold on to them. "For with God nothing shall be impossible." (Luke 1:37)

Finally I know that when I see Danny again, there will be wonderful surprises awaiting me. I am at peace. In the name of Jesus Christ, AMEN.

UNDERSTANDING THE HEALING PROCESS: ACCEPTANCE AND HOPE IN CHRIST

By Benjamin E. Payne and Heather T. Payne

Grief does not always progress in an orderly fashion. It can be unpredictable and overwhelming, but the only way to resolve it is to face it and experience it. Paul wrote in Hebrews, "Let us run with patience the race that is set before us." (Hebrews 12:1) It is not uncommon to revisit previous phases of the healing process many times. Each time can bring new feelings, understanding and awareness.

Part of the challenge of going through this process is that it also causes us to take a look at our beliefs, beliefs about our self, about God, about life, about our loved one, about our faith in Jesus Christ. As we prayerfully seek answers to the conflict that we feel inside, this opens the way for Christ to teach us. When we are taught through the Spirit of the Lord, our reexamination helps us to accept and receive hope for the future. The two stories shared above illustrate this learning process.

As you progress through the phases of healing you will begin to accept your loss and look to the future. You will still have periods of sadness and feel the loss of your loved one, but you will feel the ability to continue on with your life and experience moments of joy. You will begin to cherish again your other family relationships.

The experiences and heartfelt testimonies shared in this book have touched on questions such as: Why me? Why this? Why now? What purpose does this serve? What about the future? Is there no other way? These are normal questions whenever we walk through the "valley of the shadow of death." (Psalm 23) It can seem too difficult to face these questions and walk forward, but with faith in Jesus Christ and His love, hope in the plan of salvation and of a purpose in all things, the healing of emotional grief does happen. Don't give up. Grieving does lead to healing and understanding. The process may feel like going through a deep, dark tunnel, but know that there is light and hope at the end of the tunnel. To heal from this hurt, we must have the brightness of hope, that the Savior will help us to see the end and beyond. Moroni, his family killed, doomed to wander alone for years, was obviously comforted by these words on hope spoken by his father Mormon:

> "And again, my beloved brethren, I would speak unto you concerning hope. How is it that ye can attain unto faith, save ye shall have hope? And what is it ye shall hope for? Behold I say unto you that *he shall have hope through the atonement of Christ and the power of his resurrection, to be raised unto life eternal*, and this because of your faith in him according to the promise. Wherefore, if a man have faith he must needs have hope; for without faith there cannot be any hope. And again, behold I say unto you that he cannot have faith and hope, save he shall be meek, and lowly of heart." (Moroni 7:40-43 emphasis added)

When we approach the Lord with our sorrows He will not only comfort us and ease the burden, but He will teach us how to turn darkness to light; bitter to sweet; anger into love and compassion; doubt into confidence; blame into forgiveness; fear into faith; despair into hope and sadness into joy. The Savior has descended below all things and can understand our every thought and feeling. Like Christ, we can gain strength from what we suffer and come to know deep and abiding joy. (Isaiah 53:4, Mosiah 14:3)

Healing requires that we be honest with ourselves. The tendency to deny our thoughts or feelings will delay or even prevent us from healing. Confide in the Lord. He understands the end from the beginning. He can teach us wonderful things that we had never supposed about ourselves, our loved one(s), about Him, and about life's meaning. One of the Savior's titles is Counselor. What a marvelous opportunity to have Him at our side. No matter what our trial may be, we will never have to walk alone. He, the

Savior, will always be with us. We are counseled by the Lord: "Therefore, let your hearts be comforted...for all flesh is in mine hands; be still and know that I am God." (Doctrine & Covenants 101:16) It is in that *stillness* that we can gain great insight and learning from God. The Lord further said:

"Verily, verily, I say unto you, if you desire a further witness, cast your mind upon the night that you cried unto me in your heart, that you might know concerning the truth of these things. Did I not speak peace to your mind concerning the matter? What greater witness can you have than from God?" (Doctrine & Covenants 6:22-23) This is how most of our answers will come.

Act on the information you receive and you will soon recognize that there is greater purpose to going through this difficult experience "than you had supposed." Just like going through the tunnel, or traveling down the road at night, we have to have enough faith that the Lord will light our way to the next bend even though we can not see the end of the road. Scripture reading can also be a source of strength.

The Lord has power to help us grow and reach our divine potential. He is keenly aware of our trials and losses and he knows what experiences will bring about our greatest spiritual well being and what we can physically and emotionally endure. He knows the finished product. We are like clay on a potter's wheel and the Lord is the potter. He knows how to shape, prune and mold us in every way so that we will be " . . .vessels unto honour, sanctified, and meet for the master's use, and prepared unto every good work." (2 Timothy 2:21)

Our trials open the way for Christ to teach each of us individually. May we each "press forward with a steadfastness in Christ, having a perfect brightness of hope . . . and endure to the end." (2 Nephi 31:20) The gospel truly can bring peace and healing in a way that surpasses mortal understanding.

HELPS FOR HEALING

As you seek to accept the death of your loved one and develop a hope in Christ you will recognize some healing has already occurred. Survivors have found it helps to keep a journal and record your thoughts, feelings and impressions. Putting words to the emotions that attend suicide can bring release and closure. A journal will help you to look back when your faith is tested and you will be strengthened by recognizing the answers you have already received. Otherwise, we have a tendency to forget the power of these past experiences. In keeping a journal, you will discover your worth, your talents, your mission, your progress in healing, and insights about suicide that may not be learned any other way. For example, you could keep a journal on the healing strategies suggested in this book.

Another helpful activity may be to make a personal history of your loved one's life including photos and accomplishments as one mother did in the previous story.

Chapter 10

THE HEALING POWER OF MUSIC

In the days following the September 11th Attack on America, music helped reignite America's spirit and comfort a mourning nation. As the scenes on TV became too difficult to watch, many of us turned to music to heal us from unimaginable wrong. When Denyce Graves, an international opera star, stepped forward to sing *America the Beautiful* at the National Cathedral in Washington, she inspired, and uplifted millions of mourning Americans. In the days following, a who's who of musicians performed on network television to summon a new sense of patriotism and raise money for victims and their families.

Scientists now say that music may offer more power to mend than we ever imagined. New studies show that listening to and playing music actually can alter how our brains, and thus our bodies, function. Doctors believe music therapy in hospitals and nursing homes not only makes people feel better, but also makes them heal faster. "Whether or not people choose to recognize the power of music, it remains a spiritual experience, a healing experience," says opera star Denyce Graves, "It can save us." ("Healing Harmonies" by Tim Wendel, *USA Weekend,* Oct. 26-28, 2001)

The Lord said: "For my soul delighteth in the song of the heart; yea, the song of the righteous is a prayer unto me, and it shall be answered with a blessing upon their heads." (Doctrine & Covenants, Section 25:12-13) Survivors have said that music gave comfort and help to them during the healing process. Music of any kind that inspires, uplifts, comforts, assuages grief, or brings peace can be manna to our souls.

Good music can provide enrichment, inspiration, consolation and aesthetic experiences throughout life. The communication of emotion and meaning through music expresses one's deepest self.

Deanna Edwards and Michael Ballam, prominent LDS musicians, have spoken on the power of music to heal the mind and body. Michael is a popular speaker and opera singer, thrilling audiences with his voice and experiences live and on recordings. He shared these ideas:

> In an extraordinary state of despair in 1931, when J.C. Penney lost 40 million dollars from the depression, he determined to take his life at the age of 56. The story is told of him coming into a room at a sanitarium to seek a means to end his misery when he heard someone singing *"God Will Take Care of You"*. It spoke deeply to his soul and gave him the resolve to recover from his deadly depression.

> George Frederick Handel, after suffering paralytic strokes, was set aside in a convalescent home and expected to die. He wheeled himself to a small organ in the building and stared at it for some time. His great desire to make music enabled him to use one finger to search out a melody. After days of pain and determination he was able to use his fingers, then his hands and feet. It was the beginning of musical therapy that would lift his spirits, heal his body and ultimately allow him to create his masterwork, *The Messiah.*

I understand these stories well. Having suffered with depression a good deal of my life, and having sought various forms of help, I have discovered the surest therapy for me: I am a musical volunteer in hospitals, hospices, rest homes, jails and prisons. I'm not sure what it does for those for whom I sing, but it does wonderful things for me. It helps me to look beyond my own challenges and to feel that I am making a difference for someone. I believe that is a deep human desire. My gospel recipe is found in Matthew 25:35-36: "For I was an hungered, and ye gave me meat: I was thirsty, and ye gave me drink: I was a stranger, and ye took me in: Naked, and ye clothed me: I was sick, and ye visited me: I was in prison, and ye came unto me."

Following the Savior's directive helps me through. Music has given me the courage and means to go into difficult situations and fulfill the Savior's admonitions, to be His hands here on earth. It has blessed me and I commend it to everyone. Those whom we serve in this way are not looking for a performance worthy of Carnegie Hall, but rather a warm heart and a willingness to serve. (Michael Ballam, personal communication)

Deanna Edwards began her music therapy ministry when she was invited to be a volunteer at a hospital. With guitar in hand, her rich voice and songs have brought peace and hope to thousands in hospitals, mental institutions, hospice centers and rest homes. She presents workshops for professionals and volunteers in the health-care industry throughout the United States and other areas of the world. She speaks about the healing power of good music:

"Music is a total experience, and we found it helped to alleviate physical as well as emotional pain. By giving patients something positive to involve themselves in, we found that attention would shift from the pain to the music, much as the Lamaze method of childbirth helps a woman in labor to focus away from the pain. We found a surprisingly large number of cases in which patients' direct involvement in music helped them through uncomfortable and difficult moments. Music is not a passive experience. It is an encompassing expression of mind and emotion and serves a unique purpose in patient care . . . 'The television set can't sing my favorite songs and hold my hand,' one patient said."

After a comatose woman responded to the singing of her favorite song, *In The Garden*, Deanna said, "I sensed a new and deep fulfillment coming into my life. My thoughts of self-concern were turning to the physical and emotional well being of others. My half-day a week (singing at the hospital) was begging to become a way of life. I was beginning to learn the language of love." Deanna became aware of the unique stimulative and sedative qualities of songs. She used up-tempo tunes for exercise sessions, which aided stroke victims. Music stimulated those who suffered speech impairments and their rehabilitation was facilitated through the use of music. More mellow music helped patients relax and let go of fears and anxieties. She observed that alleviation of fear and pain was most often the result.

> "Music is a language of love and release. It intensifies, reminds, beautifies, teaches, saddens, gladdens, enlivens, and pervades all human life. It can help unite a family, heal a broken heart, and inspire an indigent spirit. It is a confirmation of our eternal existence." (Deanna Edwards, *Music Brings My Heart Back Home, pp 25, 35,*© Shadow Mountain, Deseret Book, 1988. Used by permission)

In addition to *Where Can I Turn for Peace,* page 129, there are hymns that are not as well known, which you may find uplifting. Some especially helpful ones are: *Though Deepening Trials,* page 122; *Lean on My Ample Arm,* page 120; *Oh, May My Soul Commune with Thee,* page 123; *O Savior, Thou Who Wearest a Crown,* page 197; *Come Unto Him,* page 114; *Come, Ye Disconsolate,* page 115; *Be Still My Soul,* page 124; *O Love That Glorifies the Son,* page 295; *Our Savior's Love,* page 113; *When Faith Endures,* page 128; and *Come Thou Fount of Every Blessing,* by John Wyeth, which is not in our current hymn book, but is sung by the Tabernacle Choir.

Several survivors mentioned that classical music helped lift their spirits. Choral works such as *How Lovely Is Thy Dwelling Place,* from Brahms *Requiem,* Handel's *Messiah,* Faure's *Requiem,* Mozart's *Requiem,* Bach's *Missa Solemnis,* and Beethoven's *Ninth Symphony* are but a few of the musical masterpieces that continue to inspire and uplift men and women through the ages.

Did you know that Ludwig Van Beethoven began to go deaf in his early twenties? He wrote the famous Heiligenstadt Testament, his Last Will and Testament, to his brother Carl in 1802 when he was only 32 years old and almost completely deaf. He said being in the presence of friends who could hear a shepherd's flute while he heard nothing brought him close to despair, "and I came near to ending my own life—only my art held me back, as it seemed to me impossible to leave this world until I have produced every thing I feel it has been granted to me to achieve. So I continue this miserable existence . . Oh, God, you look down on my inner soul, and know that it is filled with love of humanity and the desire to do good . . . Urge your children to follow the path of virtue, as that alone can bring happiness—money cannot. I speak from experience, as virtue alone has sustained me in my misery, and it was thanks to virtue, together with my art, that I did not end my life by committing suicide. Farewell, and love one another." (*Ludwig Van Beethoven*, page 21, edited by Joseph Schmidt-Görg and Hans Schmidt. Beethoven-Archiv-Bonn)

The Lord said: "For my soul delighteth in the song of the heart; yea, the song of the righteous is a prayer unto me, and it shall be answered with a blessing upon their heads." (Doctrine & Covenants, Section 25:12-13) Survivors have said that music gave comfort and help to them during the healing process. Music of any kind that inspires, uplifts, comforts, assuages grief, or brings peace can be manna to our souls. Beautiful music can provide enrichment, inspiration, consolation and aesthetic experiences throughout life. The communication of emotion and meaning through music expresses one's deepest self.

Great masterpieces of music, art and literature are often born from the trials and suffering of the composer, artist, or writer. Grief can push us to give expression to our deepest feelings in many creative ways, in music, poetry, literature and art.

CREATIVE USES OF GRIEF

Martin Gray, who survived the horrors of the Holocaust, later lost his wife and four children while they were attempting to escape a fire on the hillside behind their home, while Martin was saving the life of a neighbor. He was encouraged to write a book about his life. The book, *For Those I Loved,* became an international best seller. He donated royalties from his book to a fund promoting fire prevention and a children's tree-planting program in France. His message is profound:

> A man must create the world
> of which he is the center.
> This can be a masterwork:
> The painting of an artist,
> The piece of a cabinetmaker,
> The field of a peasant,
> The symphony of a composer,
> The page of a writer.
> It can be a family.
> And when tragedy comes,
> as it will, we must take this
> suffering into our hands
> and, through willpower,
> transform it into a fruit
> that will nourish us
> as we begin life again.
> This is the fragile miracle
> Hidden within us all!

(David Douglas Duncan, *The Fragile Miracle of Martin Gray)*

Deanna Edwards recounts the story of Martin Gray in her book *Grieving: The Pain and the Promise* and asks the question "How can we create with grief?" She said: "Grief creates a tremendous amount of energy (which) if left unharnessed, can wreak havoc with the mind and body or open the floodgates to a richer experience in living. The source of that energy is love . . .

Grief changes us. Our creative response to that change is the fragile miracle, hidden within us all. 'Creative grief' is nothing more than the power of loneliness and the power of love coming together to make something beautiful! Creative grief serves a far greater purpose than mere self-fulfillment. He who can see something beyond his own loss may inadvertently find a cause greater than himself---greater than the pain . . . For Christ, the gift of Eternal Life he was giving to us all was greater than the pain of the crucifixion. He never lost sight of the vision---the purpose shining above his own suffering!"(pp. 181-182)

The process of using your pain to make something of lasting value with it doesn't need to be monumental. Keeping a journal, a scrapbook of your loved one, a display in your home, planting a rose or a new flower garden, writing a song, poem or story can be meaningful. Some survivors in this book became involved in grief counseling and service projects. These creative activities provide healing therapy. Exploring your feelings and recreating those feelings in music, literature, poetry, letters, or journals, helps you to identify and define what you already know! Cliff Edwards, Deanna's husband, said: "We don't know what we know until we write it down."

"Grief means something good, only if it changes us for the better and strengthens us," Deanna observed, "The added dimension of creative grief is that as we use it to clarify and define our feelings, we gain an increased awareness of others. *The unbearable becomes more bearable when it is shared.* It is that refiner's fire that challenges us to call upon the divine within ourselves and to invite the comfort and presence of the Holy Spirit when we need it most. *Creativity is the essence of life and the evidence of immortality!* As we suffer, creativity can turn tragedy to triumph. We can testify of the ultimate nobility of the human spirit. The pain becomes a tool to create something better in our lives rather than a weapon to hurt or punish us. What we create can be shared with others long after we have passed from man's frail mortal environment. The beauty of this principle is that we can also take our creative capacity with us in to the eternal worlds." (Deanna Edwards, *Grieving: The Pain and The Promse* pp. 181-184 Covenant Communications Inc. Used by permission)

Chapter 11

"COMFORT YOURSELVES TOGETHER"
(1st Thessalonians 5:11)

Grief is experienced by all survivors of suicide. Grief is not bad, nor is it a sign of weakness or something to avoid. Grief is a necessary part of the process of healing. If there is love and joy in life, there will be grief and sorrow at the loss of those we care for. Every person experiences the process at a different pace and to a different degree. The intensity of grief associated with suicide is influenced by a variety of factors, including the quality of the relationship the survivor had with the suicide victim and the role the suicide victim played in the family. The age and gender of the survivor and the survivor's social, emotional and spiritual resources affect the course of healing. This chapter focuses on the last three factors.

IT'S OKAY FOR A MAN TO CRY
Differences between men and women

By Margie Holmes

In some ways, men and women inhabit different worlds from the time they are born. Boys are expected to be strong, active, brave, rational and independent, whereas girls are expected to be sensitive, cooperative, nurturing, emotionally expressive, and tender. Many people believe that these differences are biologically based, whereas others believe that they are learned through such means as observation, imitation, and reinforcement of sex-stereotyped behavior. Most likely both nature and nurture and the complex interaction between them throughout life influence what men and women think, feel, and do. Whatever the reasons for the differences between the average man and the average woman, during the grieving process these differences often become apparent and they can make it difficult for husbands and wives to help each other when they need it most. In addition, because emotions are central to the grieving process, men may face more difficult challenges than women due to cultural expectations and the fact that they usually spend more time in the workplace.

Friendships and feelings

Girls and women tend to be more concerned about relationships and staying connected to others. As a result, they have more close friends than boys and men (on average). They tend to talk more about how they are feeling and to provide emotional support for one another. Boys and men, on the other hand, are more likely to focus on doing things together and their conversations are less personal. When something as tragic as a suicide occurs, many men are not sure how to help their friends or family deal with such an emotional trauma or how to reach out for help for themselves. Of course, women have difficulty as well, but they often have circles of friends who are more familiar with talking about feelings. I described the support that I received from women friends in an earlier section ("What I Gained from Losing Brian"). My husband, Blair's, experience was very different from mine, as he describes below:

> Many women came to our home to share my wife's grief, but from the day of my son's death until the memorial service a week later, the bishop and another man who came with his wife were the only men who appeared. We did not see his counselors, our home teachers, any of our immediate male neighbors, nor anyone from my priesthood quorum. One father, who lost his son thirteen years previous to our son's death, told us that he drove to our home, but was unable to get out of the car and come to our door due to his own resurrected grief. I often wondered what was wrong with me that almost no one would talk to me. I thought that perhaps I was unworthy of comfort or that no one cared for me.

Grieving and the workplace

In the competitive world of paid work, efficiency and rationality are highly valued and rewarded and personal problems are expected to be kept from interfering with the task at hand. Healing from a suicide can be very difficult for both men and women in an atmosphere where emotions must be suppressed. In addition, working in a competitive setting can make it dangerous to reveal vulnerabilities because of the fear that they will be used to take advantage of the one who discloses them. This is one of the reasons that some persons keep their feelings to themselves. When the situation calls for openness and intimate connection, it can be hard to "shift gears" into what may be an unfamiliar and uncomfortable way of relating to others. Bob Rosenberger, a bereaved parent, explained that his first instinct was not to show his pain. He said, "When I learned my son died, I flew out to the city where he was attending college and made the necessary (funeral) arrangements. Then I called my boss to let him know that we would be staying over one night and I would be back to work the next day!"

My husband, Blair, found little support for his grieving process at work. He said:

> I knew that some of my colleagues attended the memorial service for Brian. Two of them came through the line, but none of the others spoke to me that day or afterward. None of them came to my office to offer sympathy. None of them, when passing me on campus, stopped to utter words of comfort. I had one good friend from outside my department who sensed the depth of my feelings and the enormity of my loss. He helped me in practical ways and by listening to me.

Occupational pursuits can be helpful in providing a respite from dealing with grief, however. When losses are fresh and pain is deep, it can be a relief to be distracted from those feelings. The regular routines of work can also help restore a sense of normalcy when our personal world has been altered forever. Unfortunately, work and other activities can also delay or prevent the strenuous emotional work that must be done to heal.

An LDS Perspective

Although LDS men have important spiritual sources of healing, they may be more subject in some ways to sex role stereotypes. Latter-day Saints are taught that there are divinely created differences between men and women. The Proclamation on the Family states that fathers are primarily responsible to provide for and protect their families whereas mothers are primarily responsible for nurturing the children. Some couples forget the additional counsel that they are to be equal partners and instead behave as though they have sole rather than primary responsibility in their respective areas. For men, this can mean limited interaction with children and few opportunities to develop the tenderness and sensitivity that good parenting requires. They become very competent in achieving goals, accomplishing tasks, and producing measurable outcomes, but may not learn to value relationships for their own sake or the skills required to foster healthy relationships. Blair expressed his feelings of regret at not being a better father:

> I had a strong sense of guilt for being a rather poor father to my son. It was difficult to think of the good things I did for him and the fun times we had. I blamed myself and wondered what I could or should have done to prevent Brian from taking the path that he did. I felt deeply worthless and severe physical pain. Grieving for my son was the hardest work, by far, that I have done in my life. I resolved at the time to go to any man I knew who was grieving to express my sorrow for his loss and to do what I could to share his burden. In that sense, my son's death made me a better person. There have been several occasions since then when I have tried to help neighbors and associates who have lost children in horrible ways. My grief and healing also made me more sensitive to my other

children's needs and more willing to draw close to them. I did not want to encounter again the difficulties that I had with Brian.

Grieving together

The different ways men and women deal with grief often brings conflict and estrangement to their marriages. Instead of supporting one another through the grieving process, they may follow different paths. She may interpret his silence as uncaring or as a refusal to deal with his feelings; he may interpret her continual tears and discussion as being unable to let it go. Instead of helping each other, they may find themselves frustrated, resentful and blaming each other for their added pain. When both partners are suffering deeply, it is difficult for either of them to give what the other needs.

I have a painful memory of sitting next to my husband at the funeral of a young man in our neighborhood. This young man was the same age as our son who had died about six years earlier from a combination of alcohol and sleeping pills. Our neighbor died of knife wounds received in a New York City subway while trying to protect his mother from an attack. He was mourned as a hero who gave his life for another. General authorities of the church spoke in his praise and the crowd overflowed the stake center. The contrast in the two funerals was vivid and I clutched my arms to my body and sobbed. I needed my husband to put his arms around me and comfort me. I couldn't understand how he could ignore my need. Looking back, I realize that he was probably trying to deal with his own pain and perhaps needed me to reach out to comfort him.

The desperate search for explanations following a suicide makes it very easy for survivors to blame each other. They may need help to communicate their feelings to their spouses and children in a loving and uncritical manner. It is healing to be honest about your feelings, even though they may seem irrational at times. Crying together and supporting each other during the bad times can bring couples closer together, but both spouses can benefit from support outside the marriage to help them through the times when their wounded condition prevents them from turning to each other. If you find it difficult to express feelings and your spouse tends to show too much emotion, try to be patient. Do your best to listen and understand the pain. On the other hand, if you express emotions easily and your spouse refuses to cry or to talk about feelings, you will need to be patient and encourage the expression of grief.

Try to talk freely about death and suicide together. Encourage one another to share memories. Attempt to create an environment where it is safe for each survivor to express grief. Pray together and pray for one another. Dealing with suicide is difficult, even in the best of circumstances.

THE SPECIAL NEEDS OF CHILDREN

Suicide can affect each member of the family in a different way. One person may grieve openly, another may retreat into silence or moodiness. Children's emotional needs can often be overlooked because the parent's grief is so all consuming. It is usually much more difficult for a child to adjust to a parent committing suicide than a brother or sister. The death of a parent brings the extra challenges of wondering, "Who will be my mom or dad? Who will take care of me now? How can I live without my mom or dad? Will my children never have a grandpa or grandma?" It is crucial for the surviving parent and other close family members to open the doors of communication with them.

The National Institute of Mental Health advises: "By talking to our children about death, we may discover what they know and do not know---if they have misconceptions, fears, or worries. We can help them by providing needed information, comfort, and understanding. Talk does not solve all problems, but without talk we are even more limited in our ability to help." *(Talking to Children About Death* DHEW Pub. No. ADM 79-838)

Encourage children to express their feelings of denial, guilt, blame, depression or loneliness. You may be tempted to 'let it ride," but don't do it. Children, like adults need to share their feelings about suicide in order to heal. Their reactions may be similar to yours. They may show anger, hurt and guilt, or seem insensitive. You need to accept their reactions, whatever they are, and give them loving support even if you don't understand them.

Children usually need some time to think about the death and to explore their feelings. Because children differ in developmental maturity, the approach taken with them must be adapted accordingly. The natural openness found in young children may make it easier for them to talk about it than an older child. Older children, especially teenagers, may have more difficulty in sharing their feelings and may require prompting. Simple explanations are best for younger children while older teenagers can often understand an adult-like conversation. Some children won't ask questions at all and you need to encourage communication. A child may react with anger, behavioral problems, psychosomatic illness and other indirect manifestations. Even normal children may express depression through anger and behavioral problems. A child or teen may not choose to act out their grief with their parents, but it is important they talk it out with someone. It doesn't matter what children talk about. As long as they are communicating you can direct the conversation toward the suicide.

Some ways to help children communicate are:
- Playing games
- Drawing pictures
- Making cut and paste projects
- Writing letters, poetry, or stories
- Keeping a journal or making a scrapbook
- Talking about memories
- Reading humorous stories
- Caring for a pet

Don't hide your grief from children. Let them see your tears and know that it is desirable to express grief. Talk about the deceased the way he really was. Verbalize how much you'll miss her. Share hope and faith in Jesus Christ and that the deceased's spirit is still alive in the spirit world.

It is critical to tell the truth and share the hurt so that the respect and love of survivors for each other can surface. Parents and relatives may think they are protecting their children by not telling them the truth, but they may see through the lie and become resentful or frightened by the adults' secrecy. Take into account the age of the child, and make your explanations simple. Children have their questions just as you do. Answer those you can and tell them that many questions cannot be answered at this time. Help children understand that their loved ones took their lives because of great emotional pain or conflict. Help them to understand that they are not the cause of anyone's death.

A child who has been exposed to suicide may come to view suicide as an acceptable way of coping with problems. Talking about other ways of dealing with problems and reassuring the child that you are interested in him or her can help prevent another suicide. Also, reassure the child that you will not choose to leave. Tell your children you cannot protect them from pain but you will support them through it.

Make it a point to talk with people the child has contact with, especially teachers. Teachers need to know what the child is reacting to and they could help you pinpoint emotional responses that may be emerging, such as a change in behavior at school. They can help you reach the child and provide additional support.

Teens (especially) need to be encouraged even more to air their feelings and not keep them locked within. They need the freedom to grieve in their own way. Parents may become overprotective and restrict the life of a surviving sibling. Teens need a verbal expression of your love, an arm around their shoulder, to be assured that you are there if they need you. It is not so important that they talk out their grief with you, their parents, but it is important they talk it out with someone. Assure them it is okay to cry, or be angry, or be lonely, but that they will heal and the pain will diminish.

Another concern that usually occurs is what is often referred to as "anniversary reactions." These are memories and feelings that reoccur with intensity on the anniversary date of the suicide. Be vigilant in preparing for these. Nearly everyone, children and adults alike will experience an anniversary reaction.

Above all, listen carefully to children and continue to find opportunities to talk about their feelings. For children who have serious problems or prolonged grieving, evaluation by a professional counselor is a wise precaution.

Other suggestions that have been found helpful are:

- Provide factual information about the death and confront rumors
- Let children assist with the details of the funeral
- Allow them to touch the body if they want to
- Develop ways to commemorate the death, but do not romanticize it
- Expect sorrowful memories to occur around the anniversary date of the death
- Have a family home evening about death
- Continue family religious activities such as attending church together and family prayer
- Arrange for priesthood blessings
- Focus on the good qualities of the individual and not the suicide

Elder Boyd K. Packer's beautiful metaphor about the hand in the glove teaches children about death as follows:

A glove is like your body. It cannot move. But when your spirit entered into your body, then you could move and act and live. Now you are a person, a spirit with a body living on the earth. While you are alive, the spirit inside your body causes it to work and to act and to live. But it was not intended that we stay here on earth forever. Some day, because of old age or perhaps a disease or an accident, the spirit and the body will be separated When this happens, we say that a person has died. Death is a separation-a separation of the body and the spirit. When the glove, which is like your body, is taken away from your spirit, it cannot move anymore. It just falls down. It is dead. But the part of you that looks out through your eyes and allows you to think and to smile, to act and to know, and to be, that is your spirit and that is eternal. It cannot die. (President Boyd K. Packer, "An Apostle Speaks to Children." Previously published in *The Friend,* July 1973. ©2000 by Intellectual Reserve, Inc.)

Understanding the plan of salvation is an essential element of healing. It is beneficial for children to know that each person, regardless of the cause of death, will live again. Suicide is not the end. A young girl wrote this poem after her father took his life.

I Miss
To my Dad, that I loved so dear.
Even though you are gone, I know you are still here.
I miss your touch, and your warm embrace.
I miss the time we shared, and your loving face.
I miss your teachings, your willful way.
I miss talking to you, and you telling me everything's okay.
I miss watching you with your granddaughter, your face aglow.
I have missed you holding your grandson,
But the one thing I know.
I will go on missing you and all your funny ways.
I will never stop loving you all my days.
Joelle

SPIRITUAL AND EMOTIONAL SUPPORT SYSTEMS: How Friends and Relatives Can Help

Many of the survivors stressed the importance of the spiritual and emotional support they received from their families, their ecclesiastical leaders, their neighbors and friends. The bishop who lost his son said: "My counselors in the bishopric did everything possible to make it easier, and there was a great outpouring of love from the ward members . . . The many sets of kind friends help me so much." In several of the stories having friends and extended family members who helped with funeral arrangements and continued to offer their support after the funeral made a difference in their progress through the healing phases.

Deanne Francis commented,

"Planning a viewing, writing an obituary and asking people to participate in a funeral are difficult, but all these things have great therapeutic value. It is the beginning of being able to say goodbye. It brings the support of friends and provides a goal or objective to work toward. It also provides for a last, loving tribute and declaration of love." (*A Heritage of Faith,* " The Many Faces of Grief," p.81, © Deseret Book, 1988. Used by permission)

To have a friend who would just listen, without offering advice, was normally helpful in the healing process. Some survivors, more than others, need an understanding and sensitive friend to whom they can disclose their feelings. The best thing others may be able to do for a grieving friend is to allow tears.

We make a sacred covenant in the waters of baptism "to bear one another's burdens . . . mourn with those that mourn; yea, and comfort those that stand in need of comfort, and to stand as witnesses of God at all times and in all things and in all places that ye may be in, even until death. . ." (Mosiah 18:8-9) This is the essence of the gospel of Jesus Christ.

This last story illustrates the importance of the survivor's spiritual resources and the value of support systems, especially family members and church officials. The loss of the father to this family did not prevent the mother or children from continuing to grow in faith and give dedicated service to the Church. Two of the children and their spouses served as mission presidents. Two of the sons have served as bishops or in the bishopric. The youngest son struggled for a while but was helped by his siblings and church leaders and has since served in many positions in the Church. The family closed ranks and was not destroyed by this tragedy. They arose from their grief with greater faith to serve and bear testimony of the Lord Jesus Christ with power and conviction.

"Our prayers were answered by loving friends and family who came and shared our sorrow."

DR. " A. "

By "Elaine"

My father was a respected physician and a very dynamic, charismatic man. Upon finishing two years of college, he turned down an appointment to West Point in order to attend medical school at Northwestern University. He was a great confidence builder for his children and all five of us loved him dearly. He had a terrific sense of humor and was a fun, fun person. It seemed to us there was nothing he couldn't do. He could even sing and tap dance far better than I. It was because of his enthusiasm and talent that the two of us won a Charleston contest when I was in high school.

He had a serious and abiding testimony of the gospel of Jesus Christ, and served in a number of leadership positions in the LDS Church. He was bishop of our ward for 4 years and served for ten years on the general board of what was then the MIA. Everything he did, however, was accompanied by debilitating migraine headaches. He taught me to give him shots of gynergen to control these headaches when I was in my teens. In retrospect, those shots may have contributed to his eventual cerebral deterioration as gynergen has a dilating/constricting effect on blood vessels including those in the brain.

He was 47 when he and mother were called to preside over a mission. My sister and I were both married and didn't go with Mother and Dad and my three younger brothers. A year later, we received a call informing us that Dad was returning to Utah for surgery on his neck, which had been injured years before and was bothering him. I picked him up at the airport and he walked right past me and didn't know me. I was flabbergasted and called out 'Dad! He turned around and said 'Oh, "Bonnie" I didn't see you!' My sister's name is Bonnie, not mine. And that was just the beginning. He did some strange things while he was home recuperating from his surgery. One day as he was grocery shopping with Bonnie, he saw a man passing out samples of coffee. Dad was the soul of diplomacy and kindness but he walked over to the man and in a loud voice gave him a resounding lecture about coffee. Bonnie was mortified. At other times he couldn't remember medications he had used for years.

In January, while still recovering from surgery and encased in a partial body cast, Dad was determined to go to our mountain cabin. Our cabin is near the high Uintas and you can't get there in winter without snowshoes. My husband John, couldn't go and I was determined Dad wouldn't go alone even though I was 7 months pregnant. We drove to the end of the paved road and parked up against a huge snow bank. As we got out of the car I realized that Dad was not dressed properly for the weather. I gave him my hat and the liners to my gloves, but he had only light pants on his legs.

It was 4 p.m. and starting to snow. Dad's judgment was badly impaired by that time in his life, but mine was fine. I was panicked at the thought of a man in a body cast and a woman great with child, each carrying 2 sacks of groceries in snow up to our waist, and walking a mile and a half to our cabin. It took us 1 ½ hours to walk to the first gate, which would normally take us about 30 minutes. After that there were no fence posts or landmarks. We wandered around lost for hours in the dark in a blizzard. Dad kept falling down and had difficulty getting up with the cast on his neck. After pulling him out of the snow several times, I took the lead. However, before long I was exhausted, had begun having labor contractions and could go no further. Dad, as always full of faith in God, directed that we should kneel down and pray, which we did, stacking the sacks of groceries in the snow. Dad told Heavenly Father he had to get back to the mission field; that I was pregnant and my children needed a mother and we needed help.

After the prayer, I (of little faith) refused to carry the sacks of groceries another step. We left all but one sack of groceries that

Dad carried and started out again. I said 'Which way should I go?' Dad said to choose any direction and it would be right. In 15 minutes I bumped into the cabin and we were able to figure out by feel which side of the cabin we were on, get the door open and go inside. I found some medication that seemed to help Dad's pain and stopped my contractions. We managed to get a fire built and stayed reasonably warm through the night.

The next morning the sun was out in a crystal sky, and we saw the depressions in the snow where our tracks went all over the mountainside. We saw the mound where the pile of groceries was, and from there, our footsteps went in a straight line to the cabin door! We were able to walk out and return home safely but we could easily have died. My dad's reasoning and judgment were gone, and his sense of humor and memory were impaired.

Another strange thing he did, was sell all of his property and assets to support himself totally on his mission. He couldn't be convinced otherwise. As a result when my parents returned, they had nothing. Dad was sick but had given up his life insurance and health insurance, which left mother with nothing. She had to work the rest of her life. We hadn't realized how serious his condition was because he was only 48. He returned to the mission field after surgery, but mother called within a few months and told us that there was something seriously wrong with Dad. He was released and the family returned home.

When Dad came home, he was so different. My brothers never really knew the 'normal' Dad that I had known. The boys would occasionally tease him and he responded like a child. He tried to go back to work for a short while, but the clinic staff became worried because he could not remember what medications he had given and for what. He did beautiful surgery but the next day he couldn't remember what he had done and why. We could not allow him to continue practicing medicine. So mother went to work as a medical secretary and Dad did a lot of temple work. He still had the awful, recurring headaches.

One morning in March, he informed mother he was going to the temple. At noon, the neighbors called mother at work and asked her to please come home. Dad had committed suicide. When she called me and said, "Dad's gone," I said, "Where has he gone?" She said: "He's dead". Knowing he was physically healthy, I said, "Wait a minute, did Dad take his life?" She said, "Yes."

If you were a physician and wanted to die you would logically go to your medicine cabinet and get the drugs to do it. But Dad didn't do that. He got a vacuum hose and put it on the exhaust of the jeep in the garage. He climbed in and turned on the motor. Our neighbors heard the motor running inside the garage for several hours, went to investigate and found Dad dead.

I drove to mother's place immediately. The police were there conducting an investigation. That evening several of the General Authorities who knew Dad came to visit us and Elder Thomas S. Monson gave the family a blessing. An autopsy was performed. President Hugh B. Brown, who had been Dad's mission president, called and asked to speak at his funeral. The night before the funeral, my husband, John, related the results of the autopsy to President Brown. The right temporal lobe, where he had headaches, was shriveled to a fraction of its normal size, while the left side was normal. The vascular headaches caused ischemia, or lack of blood flow to his right temporal lobe, causing it to atrophy. The official diagnosis was Neiman Picks Disease, which is so rare that it was afforded only a short paragraph in the neurology book we consulted.

President Brown said he appreciated that medical information because he felt Dad would never have taken his own life if he were in his right mind. In his address at the funeral, he told of the autopsy and informed the congregation that he knew and loved Dad as well as his own son, and was sure that he would not take his own life if he had all of his faculties. He said: "I would like to dispel from the minds of anyone . . . as to the nature of his passing. I have talked to the doctors who performed the autopsy . .

.and his brain could not function normally at the last, and therefore he was not in any way responsible for the act, which terminated his life. Let there be nothing said of that anymore . . . There was nothing of mediocrity about this man . . . Many things have been said to dispel the sadness and to give you courage, hope and inspiration to carry on . . . I pray that we may have nothing but gratitude in our hearts for the privilege of having known him, for the privilege of having been inspired by him, for every life he touched was blessed and benefited by his touch, and there were thousands." (Quote from funeral sermon of Dr. A. Used by permission of his daughter.)

Elder Thomas S. Monson told of Dad's years of service to mankind through the Church and the medical profession. He said there were many who would mourn his passing. He indicated that the Lord would take into account Dad's many years of faithful service. "He was one of the great and noble souls of our Heavenly Father...His soul rests in Paradise, in a place of peace and rest . . . You through your covenants and your faithfulness shall dwell eternally together (with him) in the celestial kingdom . . . I testify that all is well with him." (Quote from Funeral Sermon of Dr. A. Used by permission of his daughter.)

President Nathan Eldon Tanner counseled the family to be comforted by the good works and fine character that Dad exemplified. He quoted a poem:

> If I should die and leave you here awhile,
> Be not like others, sore, undone,
> Who keep long vigils by the silent dust and weep.
> For my sake, turn again to life and smile.
> Nerving thy heart and trembling hand to do something
> To comfort weaker hearts than thine.
> Complete there dear, unfinished tasks of mine,
> And I perchance may therein comfort you.
> (Author unknown)

The family was comforted when Church officials informed Mother that Dad should be buried in his temple clothes.

I recall Dad saying, "I am so useless, you probably would be better off without me." If any of us had ever had an inkling that he was in such pain that he would take his life, we might have paid a lot closer attention, but we couldn't believe it just because of the person he had been when he was rational.

When Dad was bishop of our ward, he counseled a woman who was suicidal, telling her that she must never consider taking her life as a solution to her problems. He wept when she later hung herself. Dad was 50 when he died but had not been himself for over 5 years. To know the cause behind the symptoms was a great comfort, which many suicide survivors do not have.

My Dad's suicide was due to a physiological disease in his brain and the words of the Apostles provided great comfort. In one way Dad knew exactly what he was doing because he took his life in a very efficient, pleasant way. But he had lost his reasoning, his judgment, his sense of humor and his memory. I think he simply cured his bad headache that morning by taking his life. We have tried to explain this to our children and it has made them more aware and empathetic. They are now more understanding of other's problems and more sympathetic to the families of those who have taken their lives.

The brain is the last frontier in medicine. It is difficult to study and to do surgery on the brain. There are electrical connections and chemical interrelationships that can disrupt the normal functioning of the brain. Dad's problem was visible. You could look at his brain and see that the right side of it was gone. But I'm sure there are things that go on in the brain that are not visible, that are microscopic or chemical that still cause a lot of problems for people. There is so much we don't yet have solutions for. If my husband had not insisted on an autopsy, we would never have known what disease Dad had.

We are counseled to take threats of suicide seriously and we should get help for that person. We don't understand exactly what is going on. Only God knows what is going on. We need to realize that the victim made a choice, wrong as it may seem to us, and we can't take the blame for the choices others make.

Prior to the onset of his organic brain disease, my father was an especially sensitive and warm individual. He was bright, upbeat, enthusiastic, and had a keen sense of humor. He was unfailingly good-natured and was adored by his patients, admired by his friends, and revered by his fellow ward members. He would often anonymously slip fifty dollars to someone who was down on their luck or, when circumstances warranted, see someone in his office and "forget" to bill them. He was unqualifiedly committed to the gospel and to the Church. It never occurred to him to turn down any kind of church calling.

His brain disease changed all that. As the disease progressed his personality changed, his judgment became flawed. His ability to remember vanished. He became an entirely different person. I believe that his decision to take his own life and his deliberate acts to accomplish that were undertaken by an individual who had been rendered incompetent by the relentless and cruel ravages of his disease. I cannot imagine that a loving and perceptive God will ever regard him as culpable. I have no doubt whatever that if I am able to remain worthy I will live with him forever in the celestial kingdom.

We are promised that through the crises of mortality, there is comfort and peace to be found if we do not "refuse to be comforted." The comforter is always there. The scriptures can always be searched. The priesthood is always available. Family and friends do reach out to share our grief and lighten our burdens. "For I am with thee . . ." (Genesis 26:24) And He was. The suicide of a loved family member is not something I would want to experience alone.

Through this very difficult time, our family learned a number of important lessons, including the value of closing our own ranks in unity. We were fortunate that each of us had a strong testimony of the gospel as a balm for troubled, grieving hearts. We clung together and reminisced and chuckled over some of the wonderful things we had heard about Dad at the funeral. We found that our prayers were answered by loving friends and family who came and shared our sorrow. Their expressions of love for Dad and their sharing of incidents from his life will always be remembered with gratitude. One couple designated Friday nights to take my mother out for a social evening. They continued doing that until her death thirteen years later.

We recognized that there are answers to all our questions even if we don't receive them now. We learned that God is just and exacting, but He is also a kind and merciful Father who meant what He said: "I will not leave you comfortless." (John 14:18)

Mother, particularly, felt a special wonder and peace in the blessings given to our family by beloved priesthood leaders. I will never forget their tender counsel and inspired words to teach us personally. It did not end after the funeral. For years, my mother received phone calls and letters – even money to help put my three brothers on missions. My brothers did not go without priesthood guidance and interviews. This has given me, personally, a deeper understanding and appreciation for the great power that there is in God's holy priesthood when it is used by righteous and inspired men.

I would not choose to repeat this experience. However, neither would I choose to give up any of the lessons learned and wisdom gained from having passed through it. Dad taught us well.

Chapter 12

WHERE IS OUR HOPE FOR PEACE?

Families that experience suicide may be uprooted from some of their basic beliefs. You are tossed on a sea of uncertainty and feel overwhelmed by a flood of sorrow. You may have a continuing struggle against the painful memories and unanswered questions. You may be haunted by the "whys," and the "if onlys." It can be a constant effort to maintain balance and keep your faith.

Even though you loved and cared deeply about your family member, you were helpless to prevent the suicide. We like to be in control of our lives and suicide takes away our sense of control. There is nothing you can do to remove it or go back or make it better. The awful finality of suicide comes as a tremendous shock. The heartbreak and pain, the shame and the stigma, cause you to wonder how you can survive these terrible realities of suicide. You may carry a heavy burden of guilt. You may worry about the spiritual status of your loved one. You may feel angry with the victim, with yourself and may even express anger with God until you find peace. You may have enormous stresses on your marriage because of the different ways some men and women deal with their grief. Some of you may need counseling and medication to help you get through the depression that can occur as a result of the trauma and grief.

Nearly all of the survivors in this book were deeply religious and committed to Christian ideals and service. This was possibly the most difficult test of all. Some questioned their relationship with God. " Heavenly Father, when I have tried to be faithful and obedient to thy commandments, why did this happen to me? Didn't you love me enough to help me save my child, my husband, my father or mother? Where is he now? Is she finally at peace? Are suicides consigned to hell? How can I find answers? Where is our hope for peace?"

HOPE

Elder M. Russell Ballard discussed the spiritual dilemmas and questions raised by survivors of suicide in an article in *The Ensign,* entitled "Some Things We Know, and Some We Do Not." He said suicide leaves many victims behind to face deep pain and confusion for years. He told of a woman whose mother had taken her life, but who received peace and understanding when she sought revelation from our Father in Heaven. She came to know that each person and circumstance are unique and will be considered individually. She felt such people have a place in the kingdom of our Heavenly Father and it is not one of despair. It is a place where they can receive comfort and peace. (Elder M. Russell Ballard, *Ensign*, "Suicide, Some Things We Know and Some We Do Not." October 1987. pp.6-9)

Perhaps the Prophet Lorenzo Snow saw our day, with the temptations and evil that threaten our families, when he gave this hopeful promise:

Therefore, mourn not because all your sons and daughters do not follow in the path that you have marked out to them, or give heed to your counsels. Inasmuch as we succeed in securing eternal glory, and stand as saviors, and as kings and priests to our God, we will save our posterity . . . God will have His own way in His own time, and He will accomplish His purposes in the salvation of His sons and daughters . . . (Lorenzo Snow Address Oct. 1893, in collected *Discourses*, 5 vols. Comp. Brian H. Stuy, Burbank Cal. 1987-1992 © 2000 Intellectual Reserve.)

President Brigham Young's words show the importance of binding our families to us by our faith and prayers:

Let the father and mother, who are members of this Church and Kingdom, take a righteous course, and strive with all their might never to do a wrong, but to do good all their lives; if they have one child or one hundred children, if they conduct themselves towards them as they should, binding them to the Lord by their faith and prayers, I care not where those children go, they are bound up to their parents by an everlasting tie, and no power of earth or hell can separate them from their parents in eternity; they will return again to the fountain from whence they sprang. *(Discourses of Brigham Young, p. 208)* © 2000 Intellectual Reserve.)

It is reassuring to know that we can invoke the Lord's help on behalf of our loved ones, as did the Prophet Alma in behalf of his wayward son. The Lord may not send an angel, but our faith in the Lord Jesus Christ will not be unrewarded. He said to "Cast thy burden upon the Lord, and he shall sustain thee . . ."(Psalm 55:22)

Elder Jeffrey R. Holland speaking at the funeral services of a good friend, who committed suicide, offered these hopeful words:

We're here to celebrate Karl's life, not his death. We're here to praise the Lord and love God for the Atonement and the Resurrection, but we are also here to say, particularly to the youth in this congregation and others who struggle, that Karl made a mistake. Now he would be the first to say that. Someone said:

> "A man to be good (and I would add a woman), must imagine intensely and comprehensively, he must put himself in the place of another. The pains and pleasures of that man must become his own. Until he can do that, he must never sit in judgment on a man or his motives."

We need a better vocabulary, Susie (Karl's wife). We know what we mean when we use the language of death, but the Master of heaven and earth, the Savior of the world, the Redeemer of all mankind, the Living Resurrection, said that when you live and believe him, you *never* die. (See John 11:25-26) So, we'll let Karl go for a while, but he's not dead in any eternal sense and you know that. You know that now and you'll know it tomorrow and you'll know it next week. You'll especially know it when he is spiritually close to you, whispers to you in your dreams, helps through the veil to raise your grandchildren-- you will know that Karl lives.

It's important to me to bear testimony to you that Karl lives, just as we testify that God lives and that Jesus lives. We testify that Karl lives spiritually and is loved of God and is loved of us. We miss him. Death was an intruder this week. We weren't ready. We do miss him and we are sorry, but none of that diminishes the brightness of his life, the grandeur of God's plan, the reality of life and the resurrection, of eternity and the Celestial Kingdom. Karl is being buried with all the promises and symbols of his covenants safely around him. God in His mercy will work out all the arrangements even as Karl works out his acknowledgement of his mistake. (Elder Jeffrey R. Holland, personal communication, August 2001, used by permission)

Elder Neal A. Maxwell, in speaking to some students at Brigham Young University, expressed so eloquently the purposes of life's challenges:

God knows what his children can become and tries them to help them reach their potential . In time each person will receive a 'customized challenge' to determine his dedication to God. ("Link Truths, Students Told Wednesday." *Daily Universe*, 7 Oct. 1983, 37:11)

And in speaking of these challenges or the "crosses" we bear, Elder Maxwell observed:

We can . . . keep moving. Crosses are easier to carry when we keep moving. . .

We can know that when we have *truly* given what we have, it is like paying a full tithe; it is, in that respect, *all* that was asked . . .

Finally, we can accept this stunning, irrevocable truth: Our Lord can lift us from deep despair and cradle us midst any care. We cannot tell Him *anything* about either aloneness or nearness.

This is a gospel of grand expectations, but God's grace is sufficient for each of us if we remember that there are no *instant* Christians. (*Notwithstanding My Weakness,* Deseret Book Co. 1981, pp. 9-11 © 2000 Intellectual Reserve.)

We come into a hostile world, subject to the imperfections of the flesh, limited understanding, and events over which we have no control. The agency of others may mean we will sorrow over a wayward family member or even a suicide.

Heavenly Father provided the power of the Atonement to lift all of us out of despair when we are confronted with mortal tragedy. The promise of hope and redemption was reaffirmed in 1918, when President Joseph F. Smith saw in a glorious vision, the work of salvation proceeding among the dead in the spirit world: "The dead who repent will be redeemed, through obedience to the ordinances of the house of God, And after they have paid the penalty of their transgressions, and are washed clean, shall receive a reward according to their works, for they are heirs of salvation." (D&C 138:58-59)

Isaiah offers you some of the most beautiful and comforting words ever penned by foretelling the mission of our Lord and Savior, Jesus Christ:

"The Spirit of the Lord God is upon me; because the Lord hath anointed me to preach good tidings unto the meek; He hath sent me to bind up the brokenhearted, to proclaim liberty to the captives, and the opening of the prison to them that are bound . . . to comfort all that mourn; to appoint unto them that mourn in Zion, *to give unto them beauty for ashes, the oil of joy for mourning, the garment of praise for the spirit of heaviness . . .*" (Isaiah 61:1-3 emphasis added)

THE ATONEMENT - AN ETERNAL PERSPECTIVE

"Encircled in the arms of His Love"

"Jesus loved his Father. His devotion was unlimited. His poise, majesty, and flawless actions among men arose from his utter submissiveness to the will of his Father. The mighty Shepherd among men was also the willing Lamb of God." (*Life and Teachings of Jesus,* New Testament Vol. 1, CES textbook, p. 43 © 2000 Intellectual Reserve)

As we come to an understanding of the Atonement of the Savior, we begin to see the trials and tragic experiences of our lives through the larger window of an eternal perspective. Christ himself has given us very personal glimpses of His atoning experiences in the Doctrine & Covenants Sections 19, 121, and 122, as He prepared His latter-day prophet for Carthage.

In Section 19, Jesus speaks of his suffering as he took upon himself the sins and pain of all mankind, "Which suffering caused myself, even God, the greatest of all, to tremble because of pain, and to bleed at every pore, and to suffer both body and spirit--and would that I might not drink the bitter cup, and shrink--nevertheless, glory be to the Father, and I partook and finished my preparations unto the children of men." (D&C 19:18-19)

March 1839.   Joseph Smith was confined in the dark dungeon of that bitter oxymoron called "Liberty Jail". He had been tutored in suffering for five months under inhuman conditions. He had survived the moldy swill, the rats, the filth, poisoning, the lack of sanitation and light, but it was more than he could bear when he received word of the Haun's Mill massacre in Missouri. The Mormons, his friends and neighbors, had been tortured, beaten, raped and murdered and were being driven out of Missouri. He cried to the Lord:

"Oh, God, where art thou? And where is the pavilion that covereth thy hiding place? . . .How long, O, Lord, shall they suffer these wrongs and unlawful oppressions before thine heart shall be softened and thy bowels be moved with compassion?... Let thine anger be kindled...with thy sword avenge us of our wrongs"

The Lord tenderly answered "My, son, peace be unto thy soul. Thine adversities and thine afflictions shall be but a small moment and then if thou endure it well, God shall exalt thee on high; thou shalt triumph over all thy foes." (D&C 121:1,3,7-8)

The Savior is asking *you,* as well as Joseph, to hang on for one more hour, one more day, one more year and to endure your afflictions well, with meekness and patience. If you will trust Him to heal you from the bitter contradictions of life, you shall triumph over your foes, whether they are physical, emotional, or spiritual. He wants you to give Him your *hearts* as well as your *heartaches*.

The Savior told Joseph (and each of us) "If thou art called upon to pass through tribulation . . . or perils of all kinds; or accused falsely; or if thine enemies tear thee from thy family and if with a drawn sword thy enemies tear thee from the bosom of thy wife . . . and thine elder son, although but six years of age, shall cling to thy garments, and shall say, My father, My father, why can't you stay with us? O, my father, what are the men going to do with you? And if then he shall be thrust from thee by the sword and thou be dragged to prison, and thine enemies prowl around thee like wolves for the blood of the lamb; And if thou shouldst be cast into the pit, or into the hands of murderers, and the sentence of death passed upon thee; if thou be cast into the deep; if the billowing surge conspire against thee; if fierce winds become thine enemy; if the heavens gather blackness, and all the elements combine to hedge up the way; and above all, if the very jaws of hell shall gape open the mouth wide after thee, know thou, my son, *that all these things shall give thee experience and shall be for thy good.* The Son of Man hath descended below them all. Art thou greater than he?" (D&C 122:5-8 italics added)

The Savior paints this scene with the pathos of His own experiences at Gethsemane and Calvary. Christ was buffeted by all the powers of darkness that Satan could unleash against Him. He endured unspeakable spiritual and physical horrors. Yet with tenderness, Jesus seems to be saying:

> "My son, my daughter, bad things also happen to the innocent and righteous to give you experience which can help you better understand and appreciate the Atonement. I have descended below them all, into the pit of darkness and despair, into hell to pay the price in blood and pain to bring you back healed and safe. I atoned for your sins *and the undeserved tragic experiences of your mortal condition.* Through your faith in me, I will bring you back healed and at-one with God."

OUR DEPENDENCE UPON CHRIST - THE PRINCE OF PEACE

Christ knows perfectly how to succor you, to comfort you, to teach and to strengthen you, but *you must initiate the power of His Atonement in your lives.* Fasting, scripture study and earnest prayer can help you gain an understanding of His atoning sacrifice. Repenting and renewing your baptismal covenants each week at the sacrament table makes you aware of how dependent you are upon Him. As you sing the sacrament hymns, the musical language of the Spirit creates a feeling of worship and gratitude. As you seek Him in His holy temple and are faithful in keeping those protective and instructive covenants, He will then endow you with His marvelous power. He said:

> "Fear not, little children, for you are mine, and I have overcome the world, and you are of them that my Father hath given me; And none of them that my Father hath given me shall be lost. . . And inasmuch as ye have received me, ye are in me and I in you." (D&C 50:40-43)

> "Be faithful and diligent in keeping the commandments of God, and I will encircle thee in the arms of my love." (D&C 6:20)

The testimonies of those who contributed to this book are significant because of their courage in sharing their honest feelings and struggles to survive the enormous test of suicide. Their words are valuable and instructive not only to other survivors, but to all who love God and are humble followers of Jesus Christ. They affirm that He lives and loves His children. They affirm the testimonies of prophets, ancient and modern. They affirm the validity of the scriptures.

A survivors support group called *Wings, (*When In Need of Grief Support-Suicide) has taken its name from this scripture in Psalms 57:1, "Be merciful unto me, O God, be merciful unto me; for my soul trusteth in thee; yea in the shadow of thy *wings* will I make my refuge, until these calamities be overpast."

These survivors encourage all who are brokenhearted and suffering to seek the unspeakable peace and comfort of the Holy Spirit, which Christ gives us midst the storms of mortality.

He said: "Peace I leave with you, my peace I give unto you: not as the world giveth, give I unto you. Let not your heart be troubled, neither let it be afraid." (John 14:21)

"But when the Comforter is come, whom I will send unto you from the Father, even the Spirit of truth, which proceedeth from the Father, he shall testify of me." (John 15:26)

"I will not leave you comfortless, I will come to you." (John 14:18)

Elder Bruce C. Hafen, in speaking of the Comforter stated, "The Comforter fills us with 'hope'...which can be literally life-sustaining when given us by the Savior, for the light at the end of life's darkest tunnels is the Light and Life of the world." Elder Hafen said the Lord will not only save you from your sins, but from your inadequacies. Many in the Church think that the Atonement is only for "big-time sinners" and that Latter-day Saints will just have to try harder and make it on their own. "The truth is not that we must make it on *our* own, but that He will make us *His* own . . . He will thus lift us up, not only at the end of life, but in each day of our lives." (Elder Bruce C. Hafen, "Beauty For Ashes*", Classic Talk Series*, Deseret Book, 1998, pp.22-23, 26 © 2000 Intellectual Reserve.)

Chapter 13

SPIRITUAL INSIGHTS GAINED ON THE PATHWAY TO PEACE

The stories in this book point out that suicide is most often not a rational act. It can be a result of mental illness, depression, a brain tumor or intense feelings of emotional pain, anguish and hopelessness. Drug and alcohol abuse was a factor in several cases. The victim was usually not choosing death as much as choosing to end unbearable pain. Sometimes there were no warning signs and even when there were, the family members did not recognize them and were not able to control the outcome. It is difficult to stop a person who is determined to end his or her life.

Ironically, suicide afflicts the surviving family members with some of the same feelings and pain that the victim experienced. Survivors experience feelings of helplessness, extreme sadness, guilt, anger and yearning for their loved one. After years of nurturing a family, it is extremely difficult for parents to relinquish their children back to our Heavenly Father. The separation is heartbreaking for the siblings too. The family desperately wants to know that their loved one is all right.

HOW THEY SURVIVED AND FOUND PEACE.

♦ They turned to Heavenly Father in humility, fasting and prayer.

♦ They searched the scriptures for understanding and comfort.

♦ They learned more about suicide, depression and other mental illnesses from reading and counseling.

♦ They read books and newsletters dealing with grief, adversity and near-death experiences.

♦ They were comforted and strengthened by friends, support groups, and ecclesiastical leaders. Many received priesthood blessings.

♦ Some received medical and psychiatric assistance.

♦ They reached out to comfort and lift others who were depressed or struggling. They served in church callings and participated in survivor support groups.

The following are excerpts from preceding chapters.

WORKING THEIR WAY THROUGH THE GRIEVING PROCESS GAVE THE SURVIVORS THESE COMFORTING SPIRITUAL INSIGHTS:

♦ **THE LORD LOVES EACH ONE OF US MORE THAN WE CAN COMPREHEND.**

"When I failed at the most important task of my life [being a mother] and found myself [still] acceptable before God and loved by my friends, it freed me up to be more authentically who I am."
--Margie Holmes

"God is the judge of each soul and the severity of each soul's trials and He is loving and merciful... I must continue on in faith and know that God loves us all, and truly wants us to come home." --Maxine Zawodniak

"While James chose to take his own life, we believe he was received by loving arms on the other side and that our Savior, who feels all our pain, knows and accepts James as the valuable child of God that he is, that his existence still holds validity and purpose."
--Arlene Ball

"Who shall separate us from the love of Christ? Shall tribulation, or distress, or persecutions, or famine, or nakedness, or peril, or sword? . . . Nay, in all these things we are more than conquerors through him that loved us. For I am persuaded, that neither death, nor life, nor angels, nor principalities, nor powers, nor things present, nor things to come, nor height, nor depth, nor any other creature, shall be able to separate us from the love of God, which is in Christ Jesus our Lord." --Romans 8:35-39

    --Kathy

◆ GOD IS AN ALL-KNOWING FATHER.

Karen Athay Packer likened her father's suicide to a beautiful ceramic bowl that he had made for her when she was a new bride. After her father's death, the bowl was shattered when they moved. She was heartbroken, but her daughter urged her to keep the pieces, because they were still beautiful. She said, "Yes, I will save all the pieces, even though I can't put them together, even though I can't make all the fragments fit. Only a loving, all-powerful Father in Heaven knows where each tiny sliver fits among the shattered remnants of a human soul."

"In our Father's healing hands, the pieces can come back together . . . Meanwhile, we can hold fast to our memories, our love, and our faith in a God who knows . . .each person's heart, each person's strengths." ("The Broken Bowl" *Ensign*, Sept. 1992.)   --Karen Athay Packer

◆ JUDGMENT IS THE LORD'S.

"Persons subject to great stresses may lose control of themselves and become mentally clouded to the point that they are no longer accountable for their acts. Such are not to be condemned for taking their own lives. It should also be remembered that judgment is the Lord's; he knows the thoughts, intents, and abilities of men; and he in his infinite wisdom will make all things right in due course." --Elder Bruce R. McConkie (*Mormon Doctrine*, SLC Bookcraft, 1966, p 771)

Elder M. Russell Ballard said the Lord was the only one who knew our genetic makeup, our state of mind, our emotional and intellectual capacities, the understanding we had of the gospel, and our physical and mental health, and He would take all things into consideration when He judged our actions on earth.
--Elder M. Russell Ballard   (*Ensign,* "Suicide: Some Things We Know and Some We Do Not."   October 1987, pp. 6-9 © 2000 Intellectual Reserve.)

"The Lord knows our hearts and is a righteous judge. He takes all of our good works into account and Dad's many years of faithful service will be noted. I cannot imagine that a loving and perceptive God will ever regard him as culpable. I have no doubt whatever that if I am able to remain worthy, I will live with him forever . . ." --"Elaine"

"And it is requisite with the justice of God that men should be judged according to their works; and if their works were good in this life, and the desires of their hearts were good, that they should also, at the last day, be restored unto that which is good . . ." Alma 41:3

♦ WE DON'T HAVE THE RIGHT TO JUDGE.

"I used to think when the Savior said not to judge that it was a nice suggestion, but now I know it is a very deep and serious commandment. We don't have a clue as to what challenges people are dealing with and we don't have the right to judge . . ."
--Marilyn Harris

"I know that we cannot judge those who commit suicide, but must trust in the loving goodness of God to deal with them in a fair and merciful way." --Arlene Ball

Elder Jeffrey R. Holland, speaking at the funeral of a good friend who took his life, stated:

God has said 'You leave this to me.' We're not wise enough to make judgments in such matters. We don't know enough. We did not walk with Karl in that dark night. As much as we have known him and as much as we have loved him, we have not been able to imagine what Karl must have been thinking. Because we can't and because God can, he has said, 'You leave this to me.' And in such times when we do not know why this would happen, then we cling to what we *do* know.

It is a great rule of life: When we come to things we do not know and do not understand, we hold more firmly to things we do know and do understand. We know that God lives and loves Karl. We know that Christ went into that Garden and to the summit of Calvary, for Karl. We know that life is eternal. We know that the plan of salvation is perfect. We know that redemption, renewal, restoration and resurrection are great principles of the gospel, great images of Christ. And so we don't throw any rocks and we don't fail to forgive. In this case, we probably aren't able even to understand. We simply yield to God in this. (Elder Jeffrey R. Holland, personal communication, used by permission)

- ## SUFFERING IS A NECESSARY PART OF LIFE'S EDUCATION

"The suffering we endure here serves to turn our hearts to God and to one another, to prepare us to go where Jesus Christ waits with open arms to embrace us and to heal us."
--Margie Holmes

"How could we expect to . . . succor those in need of succoring if we have never suffered the pain, the contradictions, the paradoxes of mortality? The Savior suffered greater contradictions than any man. Through these difficult experiences we learn compassion and understanding. If everything was easy we would never know how to 'lift up the hands that hang down and strengthen the feeble knees.'" (D&C 81:5) --Marilyn Harris.

"Out of pain often comes a finer spirit. Some better 'self' seems to rise up out of us. As we are touched by that fineness of spirit, we want to do what's right. We want to help others. We want to be tender, and kind and loving." --"Shirley"

"No pain that we suffer, no trial that we experience is wasted. It ministers to our education--to the development of such qualities as patience, faith, fortitude and humility. All that we suffer and all that we endure, especially if we endure it patiently, builds up our characters, purifies our hearts, expands our souls and makes us more tender and charitable, more worthy to be called the children of God. *It is through sorrow and suffering, through toil and tribulations that we gain the education that we came here to acquire and which will make us more like our Father and Mother in Heaven.*" --Orson F. Whitney (Spencer W. Kimball *Tragedy or Destiny,* p.4, Deseret Book, 1977,© 2000 Intellectual Reserve. emphasis added)

"One of the hardest things I ever went through in my life, taught me to acknowledge the hand of the Lord in all things---even in the trials I was undergoing. At this very trying time, I was given a blessing that told me, 'there is a fullness of the Lord's gifts, both of the Spirit and of the priesthood, which fullness is reserved unto those who come up through affliction, who love where others would hate, who respond where others would withdraw, who endure where others would give up, who forgive and embrace when others would retaliate, and who in sum, emulate through the most profound trials the forgiving and redeeming power of the Lord Jesus Christ. But thank the Lord Jesus Christ, and the power that He generated in Gethsemane, those powers of the world, the flesh, and the devil, are to be overcome.' So, why do we have to suffer? -Because we have to learn for ourselves, the fullness of his (Christ's) gift." --Gracia N. Jones. (Personal letter used by permission)

◆ THE STRESSES A SUICIDE PLACES ON MARRIAGE AND FAMILY RELATIONSHIPS CAN BE SURMOUNTED.

"One of the most difficult aspects of Brian's death for me was the wedge it drove between me and my husband. Our wounds were so deep and our vulnerability so great that we were unable to be sources of strength for one another. Our paths of grieving and healing were separate . . . I had to learn to forgive him and myself for immaturity, lack of wisdom and all of the other weaknesses that are overcome only through experience . . . All of us sin and fall short of the glory of God. . . We are all in need of God's grace, His love and His mercy." --Margie Holmes.

"I tend to be reclusive, especially if I'm hurt, so I retreated into a shell. This was very hard on my husband, but he tried to be understanding and supportive. It frightened him and the other children when they came home to find me still in my nightgown, hair uncombed, sitting in the television room watching "Geraldo," eating junk food, and sobbing that I had nothing left to live for . . . In February, my husband and I attended the temple . . . Finally, I was able to rise above my own grief and try to support and empathize with my family and friends." --Arlene Ball

◆ IN ORDER TO HEAL WE MUST FACE OUR HUMAN LIMITATIONS AND FORGIVE THE SUICIDE VICTIM AND OURSELVES.

"I must face these mistakes with brutal honesty in order to heal. I know that there is a fine line between honesty and eternal self-punishment and I am trying to forgive myself. I wanted to be a good mother. I wanted the best for my son. His choice was not my choice." --Arlene Ball

◆ WE NEED TO REACH OUT TO COMFORT OTHERS

"We, as God's children need to open our hearts to those who feel they don't fit in. Gary longed for acceptance by the neighbors and other ward members, but he never felt it. As with so many, the nicest things said about him were said after he died."

--"The Bishop"

"We as a family ask all families to show each other a little more love today, in honor of our precious son, and cling to life as a gift from God." --Arlene Ball

♦ REMEMBERING THE GOOD ABOUT OUR LOVED ONE HELPS IN THE HEALING PROCESS.

"We should not use the word 'waste' when we speak of Cory's life . . .Who are we to judge the quality of a life by the length of it? Cory's life has been full of excellence, beauty, accomplishment, laughter, joy and goodness. He fulfilled a fine mission." --"Shirley"

"I was prompted by the Spirit to compile a book on Danny's life for each of us. Working on this Danny Book was a healing therapy in my life. Page after page captured Danny the baby and his innocence, Danny the boy and his flowers, Danny the youth and his searching, and finally Danny the man and the masks. The book was a sad project, but it helped me to look at the whole of Danny's life. Slowly the tragic end ceased to swallow up everything else. Now the book is a treasure for us all."

--Jane Ann Bradford Olsen

"I pray that we may have nothing but gratitude in our hearts for the privilege of having known him, for the many things that have been said to dispel the sadness and to give you courage, hope and inspiration to carry on ... for the privilege of having been inspired by him, for every life he touched was blessed and benefited by his touch, and there were thousands." --President Hugh B. Brown, (funeral service of "Dr. A" Used by permission.)

"He (Nathan) wanted everyone who came to the funeral to take home an orange in remembrance of him. He hoped they would think of the sweetness of their friendship with him. Nathan was such a giving person, always willing to help others. His life had meaning and we hoped the orange would remind them of all the good things Nathan did in his short life." --Laura Toomey

"We clung together and reminisced and chuckled over some of the wonderful things we had heard about Dad at the funeral. We found that our prayers were answered by loving friends and family who came and shared our sorrow. Their expressions of love for Dad and their sharing of incidents from his life will always be remembered with gratitude." --"Elaine"

"Remember me for the years we had together: my smiles, my favorite food, my favorite hobby, and all the fun times we had. Things will work out. I'll be okay. You can make it. Just try. One day at a time. And if that is too hard try one hour at a time."
–Guerry

♦ MANY RECEIVED ASSURANCE OF THE WELL-BEING OF THEIR CHILD OR FAMILY MEMBER.

"We have the comfort of knowing that our Savior loves us and He loves Nathan. We feel an inner peace now that he is there. We know that our Savior has felt the sorrow we now are feeling. We know that through our Savior's sacrifice in the Atonement, we may repent, and strive to live the best we possibly can. Most importantly, we know that our family is sealed together forever, and nothing can break that chain." --Laura Toomey

"[Heavenly Father] judges us more wisely than we judge ourselves . . . His Father in Heaven loves Matt and I believe welcomed him home. I have pleaded and prayed for answers and this is the answer and peace I continue to receive." --Jean Hall.

"Dan was God's child and I cannot believe God or Jesus would want him to fail. I believe that Dan will be given opportunities now to work and advance. He believed in God and Jesus Christ." --Maxine Zawodniak

"I believe it is within the realm of each family who goes through this experience to receive their own personal witness of the well-being of their loved one." --Jane Ann Bradford Olsen

"I know that I will see my father again someday. Until that time, I feel he is in a wonderful place being counseled and nurtured by those who can care for him and teach him, helping him to conquer obstacles he could not overcome here. What a wonderful day I look forward to at the resurrection, when I can have the chance to be with him and know him for the person he truly is." --Karen Athay Packer ("The Broken Bowl*" Ensign*, Sept. 1992)

♦ **BLESSINGS AND GROWTH HAVE COME FROM THIS EXPERIENCE.**

"This experience and trial have brought our family closer together. Our children show a deeper love and respect to their parents and each other. We express that love and appreciation for one another more consistently. We are grateful to our Father in Heaven for each new day. We thank Him for the little miracles in our lives that confirm Nathan is OK . . . I find comfort in talking with those who are faced with depression . . . A simple hug or smile can make a big difference in someone else's life."
    --Laura Toomey

"I have learned to be understanding and that we need to be infinitely more sensitive to other people . . . There are people I have been able to help because I have an understanding of suicide. Another thing I have learned is the place of pain and suffering in the eternal scheme . . .that it is necessary for us to be tried . . . and God will feel after you . . . and wrench your very heart strings. . . that through these difficult experiences we learn compassion and understanding. I have had a great soul-stretching experience in life learning not to cast any stones and how to love in a divine way."
    --Marilyn Harris

"I humbly testify that challenges and afflictions in my life have brought me closer to Jesus Christ. For this reason, I consider

them to be a blessing. I also know that the Savior strengthened me for those challenges that were meant to be an instrument for my growth. I have been guided through my trials and tests and have received a greater vision and deeper appreciation for the suffering and sacrifice of my Savior, Jesus Christ and a greater desire to be more sensitive and aware of the suffering of others."
--Jane Ann Bradford Olsen

Elder Neal A. Maxwell offers these insights on the purposes of adversity:

"Human suffering does not automatically produce sweetness and character unless meekness is present. Meekness is the mulch that must go in the soil of adversity in order for empathy to grow and in order for character to grow. Jesus could not have become the most empathetic person had he not been the most meek person."

"The thermostat on the furnace of affliction will not have been set too high for us—though clearly we may think so at the time. Our God is a refining God who has been tempering soul-steel for a very long time. He knows when the right edge has been put upon our excellence but also when there is more in us than we have yet given."

"Righteous sorrow and suffering carve cavities in the soul that will later become reservoirs of joy." (Elder Neal A. Maxwell, *The Neal Maxwell Quote Book,* Bookcraft Pub. *pp.208, 7,* 335, © 2000 Intellectual Reserve.)

◆ HEALING POWER COMES THROUGH UNDERSTANDING CHRIST'S ATONEMENT.

"I remember standing at the foot of his casket when the realization came to me that he was just 33 years old, the same age the Savior was when he died and I had a great feeling of empathy for our Father in Heaven who had watched His Son die on the cross." --"The Bishop"

"Part of the healing process is knowing we have the opportunity to cast our burdens on the Savior. He said He would carry our burdens. I wasn't a perfect father because of the limitations of mortality, but the closer we are to the Lord, the less those mistakes become disasters. The Lord helps us to understand and overcome the harmful effects." --Dr. "C"

"You will not be able to believe me now. But when your depression lifts, you will have a greater compassion for the Savior and His atoning sacrifice in Gethsemane where he descended below all human suffering. He knows and understands your suffering!" --"Shirley"

"I came to understand that Christ's atonement applies to me, to my son, to my husband--not just to others. I did everything I knew how, and it wasn't enough. That's why we have our Savior . . . I can love others because I am so grateful for the love that has been extended to me and I want to return it. I can hold the hands of my fellow-sufferers." --Margie Holmes

"We will have our [son and] brother! And how is it possible? It is possible because of the suffering of Jesus Christ; because He entered the Garden of Gethsemane, because He went lower than we can comprehend, because in His agony in His lying on the ground in the blood which came from every pore, there was a place of suffering for us in our family. I don't understand, but I have faith, and the Spirit comforts me. I thank my Savior this day for His love and His mercy." --Ronny Olsen

President Boyd K. Packer in his 1995 October Conference address entitled "The Brilliant Morning of Forgiveness" spoke these hopeful and comforting words on the significance of the Atonement of Jesus Christ:

> The gospel teaches us that relief from torment and guilt can be earned through repentance. Save for those few who defect to perdition after having known a fullness, there is no habit, no addiction, no rebellion, no transgression, no

offense exempted from the promise of complete forgiveness. . . To earn forgiveness, one must make restitution. That means you give back what you have taken or ease the pain of those you have injured. But sometimes you *cannot* give back what you have taken because you don't have it to give back. . . Your repentance cannot be accepted unless there is restitution . . . Restoring that which you cannot restore, healing the wound you cannot heal, fixing that which you broke and you cannot fix is the very purpose of the atonement of Christ.

When your desire is firm and you are willing to pay the "uttermost farthing", the law of restitution is suspended. Your obligation is transferred to the Lord. He will settle your accounts. I repeat, save for the exception of the very few who defect to perdition, there is no habit no addiction, no rebellion, no transgression, no apostasy, no crime exempted from the promise of complete forgiveness. That is the promise of the atonement of Christ.

How all can be repaired, we do not know. It may not all be accomplished in this life. We know from visions and visitations that the servants of the Lord continue the work of redemption beyond the veil. (see Doctrine & Covenants 138)

President Packer quoted President Joseph F. Smith who commented on the mission of the Savior:

"Jesus had not finished his work when his body was slain, neither did he finish it after his resurrection from the dead; although he had accomplished the purpose for which he then came to the earth, he had not fulfilled all his work. And when will he? Not until he has redeemed and saved every son and daughter of our father Adam that have been or ever will be born upon this earth to the end of time, except the sons of perdition. That is his mission." (Joseph F. Smith, *Gospel Doctrine* 5th ed., 1939. p. 442)

"There is never a time," the Prophet Joseph Smith taught, *"when the spirit is too old to approach God. All are within the reach of pardoning mercy, who have not committed the unpardonable sin."* (Teachings of the Prophet Joseph Smith, page 191.) *(Ensign,* November 1995, pages 18-21© 1995 by Intellectual Reserve Incorporated.)

"I beheld that the faithful elders of this dispensation, when they depart from mortal life, continue their labors in the preaching of the gospel of repentance and redemption, through the sacrifice of the Only Begotten Son of God, among those who are in darkness and under the bondage of sin in the great world of the spirits of the dead. The dead who repent will be redeemed, through obedience to the ordinances of the house of God. And after they have paid the penalty of their transgressions, and are washed clean, they shall receive a reward according to their works for they are heirs of salvation." (Doctrine & Covenants 138:57-59)

In Revelation, John describes the glorious reunion of the Savior with His Saints. It is your invitation to press forward with faith in Christ and rely on His mercy and merits to heal you from the tragic experiences of mortality. With the Prince of Peace by your side you may overcome the searing effects of suicide and obtain hope and joy in His promise of redemption. Surely, this promise is given to both men and women, sons and daughters of Jesus Christ.

"And I heard a great voice out of heaven saying, Behold, the tabernacle of God is with men, and he will dwell with them, and they shall be his people, and God himself shall be with them, and be their God.

And God shall wipe away all tears from their eyes; and there shall be no more death, neither sorrow, nor crying, neither shall there be any more pain: for the former things are passed away.

And he that sat upon the throne said, Behold I make all things new.

And he said unto me, write: for these words are true and faithful. And he said unto me, It is done.

I am Alpha and Omega, the beginning and the end. I will give unto him that is athirst of the fountain of the water of life freely.

He that overcometh shall inherit all things; and I will be his God and he shall be my son." (Rev. 21:4-7)

A SOLITARY WAY

There is a mystery in human hearts,
And though we be encircled by a host
Of those who love us well, and are beloved,
To every one of us, from time to time,
There comes a sense of utter loneliness.
Our dearest friend is "stranger" to our joy
And cannot realize our bitterness:
"There is not one who really understands,
Not one to enter into all I feel;"
Such is the cry of each of us in turn,
We wander in a solitary way.
No matter what or where our lot may be;
Each heart, mysterious even to itself,
Must live its inner life in solitude.

And would you know the reason why this is?
It is because the Lord desires our love.
In every heart He wishes to be first.
He therefore keeps the secret key to Himself,
To open all its chambers, and to bless
With perfect sympathy and holy peace
Each solitary soul, which comes to Him.
So when we feel this loneliness, it is
The voice of Jesus saying, "Come unto me."
And every time we are not understood,
It is a call to us to come again.
For Christ alone can satisfy the soul,
And those who walk with Him from day to day
Can never have a solitary way.

And when beneath some heavy cross you faint,
And say, "I cannot bear this load alone,"
You say the truth; Christ made it purposely
So heavy that you must return to Him.

The bitter grief, which "no one understands,"
Conveys a secret message from the King,
Entreating you to come to Him again.
The Man of Sorrows understands it well
In all points tempted He can feel with you
You cannot come too often, or too near,
The Son of God is infinite in grace.
His presence satisfies the longing soul,
And those who walk with Him from day to day
Can never have a solitary way.

-Author unknown

APPENDIX: Helps and Resources
HERE'S HELP: CRISIS RESOURCES

National hot lines in U.S.
1-800-SUICIDE (1-800-784-2433) National Hotline
1-800-621-4000 National Adolescent Suicide Hotline

BEFRIENDERS INTERNATIONAL
Befrienders International is a network of hundreds of befriending centers world-wide. These centers are run by trained volunteers and offer a service, which is free, non-judgmental and completely confidential. People are befriended by telephone, in face-to-face meetings, by letter and by email. The Befrienders has an excellent listing of resources for those who may be contemplating suicide! A list of crisis centers in United States, Canada and other countries is available. Suicide resources from Armenia to Zimbabwe are provided. This site is available in different languages. The Befrienders International also provides the world's most comprehensive suicide referral Website with over 1,700 suicide helplines and emotional first aid centers worldwide and on the Internet. The main office is in London England.

Befrienders International
26/27 Market Place
Kingston upon Thames
Surrey KT1 1JH
United Kingdom
Phone: +44(0) 20 8541 4949
Web site: www.suicide-helplines.org

AMERICAN ASSOCIATION OF SUICIDOLOGY
American Association of Suicidology is a nonprofit organization dedicated to the understanding and prevention of suicide. This site is designed as a resource for anyone concerned about suicide, including, suicide researchers, therapists, prevention specialists, survivors of suicide, and people who are themselves in crisis. A list of resources available in the United States is provided.

American Association of Suicidology
4201 Connecticut Avenue, NW
Suite 408
Washington, DC 20008
Phone: (202) 237-2280
Web site: www.suicidology.org/

GENERAL SUICIDE RESOURCES

Hidden Treasures Foundation **(HTF)** is a private non-profit volunteer organization committed to carrying a message of hope. It serves as a great resource for all interested people, both professional and non-professional. HTF provides an on-line library with step-by-step instructions for accessing over 10,000 resources related to social and emotional concerns. Resources come from a variety of locations including: National and international mental health organizations; professional mental health journals; listings of support groups for social and emotion concerns; internet libraries; and finally, numerous resources tailored for members of The Church of Jesus Christ of Latter-day Saints. HTF has no paid employees. All services are managed and monitored by volunteers. HTF does; however, accept free-will donations and those interested can become sustaining members of Hidden Treasures Foundation. For more information the on-line library can be located at MentalHealthLibrary.info.

Hidden Treasures Foundation
2550 Washington Blvd. Suite 103, Ogden, Utah 84401
Phone: (800) 723-1760

AMERICAN FOUNDATION FOR SUICIDE PREVENTION
American Foundation for Suicide Prevention (AFSP) was formed in 1986, a number of leading experts on suicide came together with business and community leaders and survivors of suicide to form

the American Foundation for Suicide Prevention. They believed that only a combined effort would make it possible to fund the research necessary for progress in the prevention of suicide. A variety of excellent resources can be found from this organization.

American Foundation for Suicide Prevention
120 Wall Street, 22nd Floor
New York, New York 10005
Phone: toll free (888) 333-AFSP (888) 333-2377
Web site: www.afsp.org

SUICIDE AWARENESS/ VOICES OF EDUCATION
Suicide Awareness/Voices of Education (SA/VE) web site includes a helpful Frequently Asked Questions (FAQ) file, general information on suicide and some common statistics, symptoms of depression, a book list and much more in an easy-to-read format. In addition questions can be asked via e-mail from this site.
www.save.org/

The Link Counseling Center's National Resource Center for Suicide Prevention
348 Mt. Vernon Hwy., Atlanta, GA 30328
404-256-9797

American Psychiatric Association
1400 K. St. N.W. Washington D.C. 20005

RESOURCES: Suggested Readings

About Suicide Utah Dept. Of Social Services booklet
Ballard, M. Russell, "Suicide, Some Things We Know, and Some
    We Do Not" *The Ensign,* October, 1987.
Bolton, Iris, *My Son...My Son: A Guide to Healing After Death,*
    Loss, or Suicide; Bolton Press, 1324 Belmore Way,
    Atlanta GA 30338

Bozarth-Campbell, Alla, *Life is Goodbye, Life is Hello* by; Compcare Pub.

Cain, A.C., *Survivors of Suicide* by; Charles C. Thomas

"Caring About Kids/ Talking to Children about Death", DHEW Publication No. (ADM) 79-838, 1979. (Single

Emswiler, Mary and James, *Guiding Your Child Through Grief*

Fine, Carla, *No Time to Say Goodbye: Surviving the Suicide of a Loved One*

Fitzgerald, Helen, *The Grieving Teen: A Guide for Teenagers and Their Friends*

Fitzgerald, Helen, *The Mourning Handbook* by Helen Fitzgerald, Simon & Schuster Pub.

Grief After Suicide, (brochure pub. By Mental Health Association, 2220 Silvernail Road, Pewaukee, WI 530722-5529

Grollman, Earl A., *Talking to Children About Death*, Beacon Pub.

Hewet, John, *After Suicide,* Wayne Oates Westminster Press, 1980.

Kuschner, Harold, *When Bad Things Happen to Good People*

Lukas, Christopher and Henry Seiden, *Silent Grief: Living in the Wake of Suicide,* Charles Scribner's & Sons, 1987

Nelson, Russell M., *The Gateway We Call Death,* Deseret Book Company, Salt Lake City, Utah, 1995.

<u>*Permission to Grieve Following Suicide,*</u> booklet pub. <u>Utah State Dept. Of Health</u>

Robinson, Rita, *Survivors of Suicide*, IBS Press, 1989

Ross, E. Kubler, *Working It Through*

Rubel, Barbara, *But I Didn't Say Goodbye: For parents and professionals helping child suicide survivors*

Sarnoff, Harriet, *Living Through Mourning: Finding Comfort and Hope When a Loved One Has Died*, Penguin Books

Smollin, Ann and John Guinan, *Healing After the Suicide of a Loved one*

SOS Newsletter, Survivors of Suicide, Inc. (A self-help support group) 2411 South Woodruff Ave. Idaho Falls, Idaho 83404 tel. (208) 524-2411

Staudacher, Carol, *Beyond Grief, chap. 8 on Suicide,* New Harbinger Pub. 1987

Suicide, The American Psychiatric Association, 1400 K. St., N.W. Washington, DC 20005

Suicide and Its Aftermath: Understanding and Counseling the Survivors, Dunne, McIntosh & Dunn-Maxim, Norton Pub.

Surviving Your Child's Suicide, (brochure) and *The Compassionate Friends Newsletter,* published by The Compassionate Friends, Inc. A nationwide support group for bereaved parents. National Office: P.O. Box 3696 Oak Brook IL 60522-3696 (312) 323-5010

Teen free copies may be obtained from: Public Inquiries, National Institute of Mental Health, 5600 Fishers Lane, Rockville, Maryland 20857)

Understanding and Coping With Your Grief (brochure pub. by SOS)

Wrobleski, Adina, *Suicide Survivors: A Guide for Those Left Behind*

Worbleski, Adina, *Suicide: WHY,* Afterwords, 5124 Grove St. Minneapolis, MN 55436

BOOKS ABOUT LIFE AFTER DEATH

Hello From Heaven --by Bill & Judy Guggenheim
Life After Life --by Raymond A. Moody Jr.
Beyond Death's Door --by Maurice Rawlings
Return From Tomorrow --by George Richie & Elizabeth Sherrill
Life After Death: Insights from Latter-day Revelation
        --by Robert Millet
Beyond Death's Door --by Brent & Wendy Top
Heading Toward Omega: In Search of the Near Death Experience
        --by Kenneth Ring
I Stand All Amazed --by Elaine Durham

AUTHORS:

Jaynann Morgan Payne

Married to Dean W. Payne, a retired attorney. The Paynes have twelve children, sixty-four grandchildren and fifteen great-grandchildren. Sister Payne has a Bachelor of Arts degree from Brigham Young University. She has lectured for CES and BYU Education Weeks programs. She was National Director of the Center for Family Studies for the Freemen Institute from 1980 to 1983. Jaynann Payne has authored several books, *Ensign* articles, and *"Family Life Lines,"* 82 weekly columns in the Manila Chronicle, for which she received the Philippine National Advertising Board's "Golden Pearl Award" for the year 1996. She and her husband served a Public Affairs mission in the Philippines from 1995-97.

Sister Payne received most of the stories in this book from close friends, who suffered the tragedy of suicide, and wanted to share their experiences with other LDS families

Dr. Rick H., Director of the Hidden Treasures Foundation.

Appreciation is expressed to Dr. Rick H. for taking an interest in this book and offering his professional expertise along with many helpful insights and suggestions. A successful lecturer and psychologist, Dr. Rick H. is the author of the book, *Hold On To Hope,* a helpful book for LDS Addicts and their families.

Benjamin E. Payne, MSW & LCSW and Heather Tippets Payne, R.N.

Ben is a licensed clinical social worker and has been a crisis counselor at two hospitals in Gridley and Yuba City, California. He is presently the Chief Administrator and counselor for "Children's Hope" a foster family agency which he and his wife, Heather, own. Heather is an RN and both have had experience helping families affected by suicide. They have been shaped by adversity as they have cared for their oldest daughter, Mariah, who suffered severe brain damage in an accident fourteen years ago. Ben and Heather have five children and are caring for two foster children.

Margie Holmes, PhD

Sister Holmes received a PhD. in Family Studies from Brigham Young University and is a Research Analyst in the Research Information Division of The Church of Jesus Christ of Latter-day Saints. She is married to Blair R. Holmes, an Associate Professor at Brigham Young University, who teaches Eastern European studies. They have six children. We acknowledge her editorial expertise and contributions. She has been a supportive and encouraging friend.

....

INDEX

Acceptance   2, 29, 43, 58, 101, 123, 171
Accountability 6, 21, 30, 74
Accountable   74, 167
Anger 2-3, 11, 24-25, 29, 45, 48, 50, 60-63, 67, 78, 97, 109-110, 124, 141, 155, 161, 165
Assurance   68, 173
Atonement   3, 6, 76, 106, 119-120, 124, 157, 159-160, 162, 164, 173, 175-177
Ballam, Michael   128-129
Bargaining   2, 29, 65, 78, 80, 96
Bill   31-32, 46, 92
Blame 2, 7, 25, 29, 45, 51, 60, 62-63, 78, 80, 103, 106, 124, 138-139, 141, 153
Blessings   3, 38, 69, 80, 95, 104, 106, 109-110, 143, 154, 166, 174
Children   1-3, 11-13, 16, 29-30, 33, 46-47, 49-50, 53, 57-58, 65, 67-70, 73-76, 80, 90, 92, 97, 105-106, 109-110, 112-114, 116-119, 131-132, 138-142, 146-148, 152, 156-158, 163, 165, 170-171, 174, 185-186, 188-189
    Communication   140-141
    Helping Children Heal 30, 138-142
    Special Needs   140
Comfort   2-3, 6, 33-34, 39-40, 51, 53-54, 63, 68, 74, 76-77, 80, 85, 87-88, 90, 93, 95, 102-104, 108, 110, 113-114, 120, 124-125, 121, 129, 131, 133, 135-137, 139-140, 145, 151-154, 156, 159-160, 162-166, 171, 173-174, 176, 186
Communicate   139, 141
Communication   13, 110, 128-129, 131, 158, 169
Denial 2, 18, 29, 31, 42-44, 60-61, 141
Depression   1-2, 6, 33-34, 39-40, 51, 53-54, 63, 68, 74, 76-77, 80, 85, 87-88, 90, 93, 95, 102-104, 108, 110, 113-114, 120, 124-125, 127, 129, 131, 133, 135-137, 139-140, 145, 151-154, 156, 159-160, 162-166, 171, 173-174, 176, 186
Disbelief   46, 102
Distress   13, 166
Edwards, Deanna   128-130, 132-134
Ferre, Richard C.   vi-viii
Graves, Denyce 127

Grief   3, 14, 23-24, 26, 29-30, 40, 51-52, 54, 60-61, 68, 78, 89, 93-94,
         97, 103, 108, 123, 127, 131-133, 135-143, 145-146, 153, 155,
         163, 165, 171, 181, 185-187
    Grieving Process Five Phases   2, 30
Growth   30, 43, 107, 118, 174, 175
"Guerry"   9, 15
Guilt   21, 23-24, 26, 30, 33, 37, 39, 50, 68, 70, 72, 76, 78, 84-86, 89,
         97, 108-109, 114, 126, 137, 139, 155, 167, 178
Hall, Jean   31, 173
Harris, Marilyn 65, 168-169, 174
Healing   2, 5, 12, 23, 25, 29-30, 42-44, 57, 63, 65-66, 79, 82, 64-
                85, 97, 98-99, 101, 106-108, 112-113, 115, 118-119,
                124, 127-129, 132-134, 139-140, 166, 170-171, 175,
                183-184
    Healing Process   2, 12, 29-30, 42-44, 63, 65, 80, 83, 85,
                           100-101, 104, 116, 123, 130, 144, 173,
                           177
Hell   25, 39, 58, 114, 155, 157, 162
Historical 5
Holmes, Margie   101, 104, 135, 166, 169, 171, 176, 189
Hope   2-4, 7-9, 15, 18, 23, 30, 42-43, 54, 59, 68-69, 75-76, 88-90, 97,
         103, 107, 111, 116, 122, 125, 127, 129, 137, 147, 153-154, 157,
         162, 164, 173, 178, 187-188
Jesus Christ   2-3, 6-7, 12, 14, 30, 40, 66, 68, 71, 78, 108-109, 111,
                 119, 121, 123, 125-127, 129, 137, 142-143, 154, 157-
                 158, 160-161, 166, 169-171, 174-175, 177-178, 180-181,
                 183
Journals   75, 106, 126, 133, 141
Judge   20, 25-26, 35, 40, 54, 59-70, 75, 88, 111, 166-168, 172,
                 174
Judgment   75, 98, 105, 108, 115, 146-147, 149-150, 155, 167
    Lord's Judgment   75, 98, 167-168
"Kathy"   9-10, 167
Linkletter, Art 5
Loneliness   2, 7, 25, 30, 57, 84, 96, 98-99, 136, 180
Love   1-2, 8-9, 12-13, 15, 18, 23-27, 29-31, 33, 35, 37, 41, 43, 45, 47-
         48, 50, 52, 58-59, 62, 68, 70-72, 74, 77-79, 81, 84, 88, 91, 96,
         98-99, 102-103, 106-108, 112, 115, 117, 124-125, 127, 130, 137-
         138, 141, 150, 154, 161, 166-167, 171-173, 175, 177, 180
McConkie, Bruce R.   39, 74, 167

Memories of Deceased 11, 41, 63, 93, 107, 135, 137-139, 151, 167
        Ways to remember deceased   107, 129, 137
Men   2-3, 135-139
Olsen, Jane Ann Bradford   108, 114, 118, 170, 174-176
Pangrazzi, Father Arnaldo   23-27
Payne, Benjamin   29, 123, 188
Payne, Heather   123, 188
Payne, Jaynann   1, 188
Peace   2, 4, 20, 33-35, 40-41, 62, 72, 77, 80, 88, 103, 111, 124, 127-
        128, 146, 147-149, 159, 161-162, 171, 184
Perdition   4, 119-120, 176-177
Prayer   14, 55, 63-64, 66, 74, 81-82, 103, 111-112, 114, 119, 122, 139,
        145, 160, 164
Punishment   5, 39, 53, 104, 171
Satan   95, 103, 105, 110-111, 115, 118, 162
Savior   15, 45, 48, 58, 72, 79, 88-89, 94-95, 99, 108, 111-112, 117,
        121, 123, 127-128, 153, 155, 157-160, 162, 166, 168-169, 174-
        178
Shame   5, 17, 26, 47, 103, 111, 155
"Shirley"   83, 89, 170, 172, 176
Shock   1-2, 23, 30-32, 36-37, 42-44, 48-49, 51, 61-62, 71, 73, 103, 110,
        112, 152
Sin   3, 6, 76, 105, 107, 116, 122, 124-125, 160, 162, 171, 178
Smith, Joseph Jr.   4, 41, 71, 95, 113, 116-117, 120, 161, 178
Smith, Joseph F.   4, 120, 159, 177
Snow, Lorenzo   156
Solitary Way, A   180-181
Sorrow   3, 44, 47-48, 68-69, 89, 91, 106, 124, 128, 137, 144, 146, 150,
        164, 167-168, 160, 172
Spirit   3, 9, 13, 18, 24-25, 27, 30, 33, 35, 41, 44, 48, 54, 58, 63, 67, 69,
        74, 80, 84, 90-91, 96, 105, 107-108, 111-115, 117-121, 124, 126,
        128, 130, 137, 139-141, 152, 155, 156-162, 170, 172, 177-178
    Conflict   2, 8, 80
    Guidance   6, 13, 105, 112-113, 151
    Pain, Emptiness & Void   10, 12, 16, 23, 42, 153
    Recovery   30, 43-44
    Sources   133, 142, 183
    World   33-35, 41, 50, 124, 137, 157
Spiritual Insights   164-166
Stigma 1, 5, 40, 42, 155

Stress   19, 67, 77, 82, 97, 118, 141, 152, 167, 171
    Marriage & Family Relations   171
Suffering   1, 8, 16, 19-20, 26, 40, 44, 51, 72, 77, 86, 89-91, 104-108, 117, 121, 134, 158, 161, 170, 175-177
Suicide   1-3, 6-9, 12, 14, 17, 19, 20, 23-24, 26-27, 29-30, 33-35, 39-40, 42-44, 46, 50-54, 61-64, 66, 68, 70-71, 74, 76-77, 81-82, 86-87, 90-91, 95-96, 99-100, 129-132, 135-139, 146, 148-150, 152-154, 156, 161, 164, 167-168, 175, 178, 182-185, 187-188
Support   2, 11, 21, 27, 30, 52, 55, 70-71, 96, 99, 103, 107, 131-132, 135-136, 138, 141-142, 145, 161, 165, 171, 185-186
    Systems   145-146
"Thomas"   56
Toomey, Laura 72, 77, 173-174
Understanding 7, 19, 25, 41, 52, 61, 64, 69-70, 79, 90, 95, 98, 106, 112-113, 127-128, 130, 137, 141-142, 150, 152, 154, 157, 159, 161, 163, 165, 169, 171, 175-176, 182, 186
Warning Signs   8
Whitney, Orson J.   170
Young, Brigham   114, 156-158
Zawodniak, Maxine   36, 166, 173